Discovering
BIRD WATCHING

Jim Flegg

D0682800

Shire Publications Ltd.

CONTENTS

ACKNOWLEDGEMENTS

I am greatly indebted to Dr Pamela Harrison for providing many of the photographs (plates 1, 2, 3, 5, 6, 7, 8, 9, 10, 15, 16, 18, 19, 21, 22) so magnificent and so appropriate to the text. The remainder of the plates are from my own photographs, chosen so that ordinary birdwatchers with a camera shall not be discouraged by the quality of the work produced by bird photographers proper! Similarly I am pleased to thank Robert Hume for the line drawings that regularly enliven the text, and the British Trust for Ornithology for permission to reproduce text figures from their booklets *Nestboxes* and *The Nest Records Scheme*.

Jim Flegg

1. WHY DO WE WATCH BIRDS?

Why do we watch birds? What is their fascination? Perhaps it is because birds are one of the commonest forms of wildlife in our surroundings, always adding to the pleasure of being alive. Rarely can we get away from birds: on the most remote Highland moor, the specially lonely and, in the circumstances, appropriate call of the Golden Plover echoes around, while in the busiest London station House Sparrows and Feral Pigeons (both much grubbier than their country cousins) abound. Because of this, an enthusiasm for birds can make dull places more interesting – routine trips enjoyable. Birds can enliven the walk to the station or to school and can add another dimension to a holiday, either at home or abroad. A detailed investigation of the neighbourhood of your home can produce as many surprises and interesting discoveries as a trip to strange areas with very different climate and vegetation, such as around the shores of the Mediterranean. Perhaps it is this most of all that leads people on from just looking at birds to the fuller and deeper enjoyment of a developing interest in studying them.

Undoubtedly there are pleasures in being amongst wild living things. This may be the close proximity of a worm-hunting Robin during the autumn digging, when every feather is crystal clear and even the least murmur of song cuts into still air, or watching a Goldfinch neatly de-seeding a teazle, or it may be

Goldfinch

Great Grey Shrike

standing in Trafalgar Square during a winter evening rush-hour, seeing the wheeling Starling hordes against the sky and listening to the traffic-drowning chattering as squabbles arise over ownership of the best roosting sites on the surrounding buildings. For those denied the pleasures of geese against an estuary sky, gulls flighting to roost in very similar V formations provide an aesthetic equivalent. Take the trouble sometime to look at one of the Starlings on the lawn – regarded by many people as quarrelsome and domineering over the food supplied: on one of those occasional warm winter days watch closely the male Starling as he sings – throat feathers bristling out, his springtime purple sheen beginning to develop. The domestic entertainment of watching Tits on the bird table can be matched by watching Fieldfares and Redwings feeding on frost-fringed hawthorn berries in a winter hedgerow – these two, in close up, have the subtle beauty that is to be found in many European birds.

The pleasures of listening are also manifold. The first song, wild and lonely, of the Mistle Thrush staking territorial claim in midwinter is always the sign of better things to come, even if there are those – both country and town dwellers – who feel that the 'dawn chorus' in spring, starting in the small hours, may be an overrated event. To walk through a quiet woodland on a warm summer morning or evening can be both a relaxing and a tantalising event: the luxury of listening unthinkingly to thrushes, warblers and perhaps the prime songster, the Nightingale, against a steady purring background of Turtle Doves can be matched by the problems of separating the song of the Blackcap from that of the Garden Warbler, as neither bird is likely to be showing itself often.

Sheer hunting instinct comes to the surface in obtaining really close views of birds – with the satisfaction of a stalk successfully achieved, perhaps capped by the correct identification of the bird. A close approach is, of course, most valuable in naming new birds – there is great satisfaction in unravelling the problems of identifying a species for the first time, and in seeing life or

4

regional bird lists gradually grow. A list of birds seen can be an interesting document, and some birdwatchers derive great pleasure in trying for a high total of species, for example in a single day (a total of over a hundred different species of bird has quite often been achieved in Britain) and there are some bird-watchers who have a life list of over three hundred different species in Britain and Ireland! Rare birds of course, like rare stamps or rare coins, do have some additional sparkle, as they present additional problems of identification, and they may have travelled phenomenal distances to be present – possibly from the USA, Asia or Arctic Russia (plate 1).

As with many hobbies, an increasing involvement leads to an increasing interest. Starting as things to be looked at with pleasure, birds can be watched more closely, and perhaps studied, and with developing knowledge comes the desire to search for more information. How do birds go about their daily business? How far does a Robin or a gull travel each day, or during its lifetime? Where do the birds we see in winter come from, or those that we see only in the summer – like the Cuckoo – go to in winter? How long do garden birds live, and what are the major threats to them – cats, cars, chemicals or old age? How many eggs do they lay, and how many of these survive to become the next generation? All of these are important questions, and

Sparrowhawk – predator threatened by pesticides

5

questions to which we need answers. They are important in their own right, as aspects of bird biology, but the answers may be of real help to bird conservation. Here and unlike many hobbies, the increasingly detailed interest of the amateur can be of considerable benefit – the birdwatcher can actually help the birds he so much enjoys watching. Not only that, but today, as in the past, birds may be the first to show the early signs that all is not well with our environment. In the past, coal miners took canaries down the pits to warn of firedamp – the canary being far more susceptible to poisoning by this gas than man himself. Today, we can regard bird populations as early warning indicators that all is not well in our environment in terms of atmospheric or agrochemical pollution, or of oil (plate 2) or industrial wastes discharged into the sea.

It is fair to say that our entire environment, the ecosystem of which man is but a part, could not exist without birds: some birds eat plants, insects or larger animals, and some themselves are eaten by other creatures. These forces all contribute more or less to a balance, and an ecosystem without birds would be as practical as a balloon with a hole in the side – it would collapse.

So the birdwatcher has a complete choice of the level at which he follows his hobby – anywhere from the pure enjoyment of just looking at birds to the still entirely enjoyable but more exercising task of finding and identifying more difficult species or of looking in a more interested way at some aspects of bird behaviour or biology. Over and above the enjoyment, he can rest assured also that all his observations may be of use to conservation. The following chapters give practical hints on bird watching, and provide an outline of the sorts of opportunities available for the more enthusiastic watcher.

Woodcock roding

2. THE EQUIPMENT

Binoculars

If there is any one essential to make bird watching satisfying it is the possession of binoculars. Distant black dots take on identifiable form and a new wealth of detail gives greatly added enjoyment even to watching birds and their behaviour in the garden – what colour, for example, is the base of a Starling's beak in summer? Knowing that males have a bluish tinge and females (appropriately enough) pinkish, how does their behaviour vary? Which of the pair is dominant at the bird table?

Today the choice of binoculars available to the birdwatcher is so much wider than even ten years ago that a simple 'consumer report' assessment is no longer possible, but the British Trust for Ornithology produces a guide to the choice of binoculars, telescopes and cameras. The range of prices is similarly wide, but most birdwatchers agree that the extra optical qualities obtained from the most expensive models do not match the amount of money spent. Similarly, some of the cheaper binoculars are structurally or mechanically weak and likely to give trouble, and some are optically poor – the picture they present is not in focus from edge to edge and the images may have coloured edges – problems due to bad lens design or manufacture. In short, other than some of the cheapest and some of the most expensive glasses, you get what you pay for! The advice of a reputable supplier is always worth seeking, and many suppliers in Britain now place their own brand name on imports from Germany or Japan. The construction, performance and servicing of glasses from these countries is much improved, and many Japanese glasses are good buys in their range.

Besides satisfactory optical performance and mechanical structure, the birdwatcher always wants binoculars that are easy and comfortable to handle and to focus, and not too heavy to wear all day. Always it is worth a thorough test of these points outside the shop, or preferably in a nearby open area if the dealer will allow it. Such a test, in the type of country in which the glasses are expected to be used most, can be invaluable in picking the type and magnification best suited to individual needs.

There are three main optical points to consider when making the choice, all to some extent related to one another. They are: magnification – that is how many times bigger the binoculars make things look; field of view – that is the width of the picture seen (this is usually measured in degrees, or in yards width at 1000 yards distance); and light transmission – as all glasses reduce the amount of light reaching the eye, this effect can be specially important in poor lighting conditions. Light transmis-

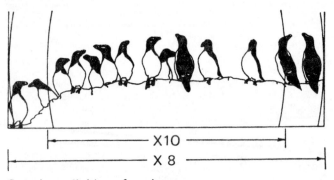

Relative fields of view

Binocular fields of view

sion is a function of the magnification and the diameter of the object lens – these are the two figures normally engraved on all binoculars, and most light is transmitted by binoculars of relatively low magnification with wide object lenses.

For general bird watching purposes, magnifications of ×7, ×8 or ×9 with object lenses of 30–45 millimetres diameter are generally considered most satisfactory. In more enclosed habitats, such as woodland where there is generally rather less available light because of the trees and leaves and also less need for high magnification as birds are often closer, ×7 or ×8 magnification and 40–50 millimetre object lenses may be most suitable, but many 7×50 glasses are rather bulky. In open surroundings – farmland, marshes, the coast or mountains and moorland, for example, higher magnifications are usually considered preferable, ×10 to ×12 being standard. Such glasses are usually heavier, and those with larger magnifications often combine unwieldy characters with poor light transmitting properties. Variable magnification binoculars are now available, although rather costly. Some birdwatchers find them very satisfactory, but such an attractive feature can only be obtained with some loss of optical quality. Rarely can magnifications over ×12, and almost never over ×15, be achieved without poor optical quality or excessive weight, and for all its disadvantages, for really high magnification a telescope is the only answer.

Telescopes

Recent telescope design has got away from the classical leather-bound brass multi-draw-tube instrument, up to a yard long when extended and requiring special skills in finding a comfortable reclining position to make its use at all possible. Today's telescopes are much shorter and lighter, usually with only a single draw tube, and focus by the turning of a small knob rather than pushing tubes in and out, but even so practice and sense are still needed for satisfaction. Being of high magnification, all telescopes transmit rather little light, and are really satisfactory only in good lighting conditions. Many have adjustable magnification between × 20 and × 40 or × 60. As with binoculars, the advice of a reputable dealer, together with a period of testing in the field, is probably the best guide to a suitable purchase. Remember that a good pair of binoculars always comes first – high magnification alone will not necessarily allow a bird to be identified and telescopes, using one eye, are always tiring to use!

Field guides

There are available several relatively cheap pocket-size paperback guides to commoner birds, or to birds of a single habitat – for example, gardens. Whilst these guides do form a part of a birdwatcher's introduction to his subject, experience indicates that they are soon outgrown, and the birdwatcher looks for more help with less usual species, and requires a rather fuller account of bird behaviour and biology. This category is also well served by relatively portable guides, but these concentrate on distribution and the problems of identification.

These guides all rely on the natural groupings of birds. Here, for example, all the ducks are described in the same section, and pictured, several at a time, in coloured plates. In the plates in the case of the *Field Guide to the Birds of Britain and Europe,* by Peterson, Mountfort and Hollom, the plates are prepared in a semi-stylised way with the main identification features indicated by pointers. Short paragraphs of description of plumage, habits, song and habitat, together with a distribution map indicating the parts of Europe in which the species occurs, accompany each species. The *Hamlyn Guide to the Birds of Britain and Europe,* by Bruun and Singer, *The Shell Guide to the Birds of Britain and Ireland,* by Ferguson-Lees, Willis and Sharrock (published by Michael Joseph), and Collins' *The Birds of Britain and Europe, with North Africa and the Middle East,* by Heinzel, Fitter and Parslow follow much the same general lines, but possess more informative distribution maps with a clearer indication of which areas are for wintering and which for breeding. In both, the plates are more lifelike than Peterson's deliberately stylised treatment, and although they do not use indicator arrows, the subsidiary sketches (better by Willis than by Heinzel or Singer) showing the 'jizz' of the individual or the flock are most helpful. Certainly no birdwatcher should be without one of these guides.

Experience and practice in the field are without question the best teachers, and no amount of bookwork can replace them. Because of this, a good notebook is essential, and in this not only can numbers, dates and places be recorded, but also notes on how the birds were identified, and possibly brief sketches. The features which strike observers may differ considerably from person to person, so a brief note or sketch on how *you* identified the particular species will always be valuable. The British Trust for Ornithology produces pocket checklists, on which details of a series of bird watching trips can be recorded.

Textbooks

There are several major works giving full details of distribution, identification, calls and song, and plumage changes through the year, together with very full details of the biology of the species concerned – its nest, eggs, clutch size and incubation period, and its measurements. The biological details make the whole study of birds more fascinating, and sometimes the measurements given can help identify a difficult corpse – such as one washed up on a beach oiled, or flattened by a car. The cheapest of these is the *Popular Handbook of British Birds*, with its sister volume the *Popular Handbook of Rarer British Birds*, both edited by P. A. D. Hollom. These two volumes are largely a condensation of a five-volume work, *The Handbook of British Birds*, edited by Witherby, Jourdain, Ticehurst and Tucker, first published in the 1930s, and long regarded as the standard work on British birds. Although the *Handbook* is still in print, only minor revisions have been incorporated, and a new work, of similar pattern but wider scope, including all the western European species, is now in preparation called *The Birds of the Western Palaearctic*. Three volumes, ranging from the divers to the gulls, have been published. Bannerman's twelve-volume series *The Birds of the British Isles* gives rather fuller details of biology than the *Handbook* together with a wealth of personal or anecdotal information on the species concerned, but is very expensive.

On a world-wide scale, large and colourfully illustrated books such as Austin's *Birds of the World* deal briefly with the habits, plumages and distribution of most bird families, but of course can only describe in very general terms representative species.

A great many monographs — books describing in detail the life history of a single species — have been written, and a selected list is given in the bibliography.

Recordings

One additional aid to identification now widely available is a series of recordings of bird song. Several such series, almost always well produced, are available on tape cassettes or 33 r.p.m. or 45 r.p.m. records; some are listed at the end of this book. In general these records are devoted to a single sort of habitat — for example woodland or marshes — and give bands of song of many of the species that the birdwatcher is likely to encounter there. To be able to recognise the songs or calls of birds can be most helpful, as very often birds are heard before they are seen, and the forewarning given by recognising the song will allow a more careful approach, and with luck a better view of the songster.

These records can be very helpful in sorting out species that are rather scarce, like the Woodlark, or normally rather shy - for example the Blackcap and the Garden Warbler, species with fairly similar songs that sing from deep in clumps of bushes. Also, they can help with probably the most puzzling pair of species in this country, the Willow Tit and the Marsh Tit. Although very similar indeed in appearance, the calls of these two are quite different and with a little bit of practice the voice is probably the best way of separating them.

Woodlark

Amateur recording of bird song is a new and rapidly developing hobby on its own, and the equipment now in use is in many cases too complex to be considered here. One very useful piece of readily portable equipment now available is a battery-powered cassette tape-recorder. These are very simple to operate, and with the microphones now available give presentable results without resorting to high-fidelity techniques, parabolic reflectors and so on. Not only can a tape of the birds seen act as a reminder of their songs, but the songs of any unrecognised species can be compared at leisure and in comfort with the records. For some species, such as the Nightingale, a portable tape-recorder has a special use. The Nightingale, master songster, usually sings from deep in a clump of bushes or brambles - even a brief recording played back will arouse the Nightingale's competitive instincts and the bird will come closer to the loudspeaker - often right out into the open. Many warblers will also react in this way, as will flocking species such as the Redpoll or just plain inquisitive ones like the tits.

Photography

One of the most worthwhile pieces of equipment that the bird-watcher can take with him is a camera - for recording events, scenery, habitats and often birds - one good way to count a flock of birds is to take a photograph of it and count it when you have time to be accurate! The ability to recall events or expeditions is always pleasurable, and the possibilities of recording details of numbers of birds, or the appearance of an unusual bird may be most valuable.

The choice of a camera is even wider than for binoculars, from simple 'instamatic' types suitable for photographs of favourite bird watching haunts through to kits costing many hundreds of pounds. Photographing the birds themselves is a most absorbing hobby, but certainly no birdwatcher should be without a camera. The BTO guide *Binoculars, Telescopes and Cameras* should help you with the choice, as it deals fully with the types available.

The great majority of cameras available use 35-millimetre film - and a wide range of films, both black and white and colour, suitable for all light conditions, is readily available. Better quality, especially in colour photography, can be obtained with 5×5 centimetre ($2\frac{1}{4}$ inches square) film, but cameras and accessory lenses, projectors and film are relatively much more expensive.

It is possible now to buy the necessary 35-millimetre camera and a telephoto lens suitable for bird work for about £150. As with binoculars, the advice of reputable suppliers is worth taking, especially concerning the servicing possibilities for foreign-made cameras.

With the advent of freely interchangeable lenses it is possible to build up a full set of equipment over the years. Thus it pays to buy one of the more usual threaded lenses, and always to buy a camera capable of accepting other lenses. Similarly, by far the most practical camera body in use today is the type known as a single-lens reflex. In these the picture in the viewfinder is precisely that thrown by the lens on the film, whatever the focal length of the lens in use.

For habitat photographs, use either a 50-millimetre standard lens or a wide angle (say 35 millimetres). For close-ups of birds in the hand it is helpful to have these focusing down as much as possible — preferably to 18 inches or less. For even closer detail a macro (close-up) lens or extension tubes can be used. For tamer birds like gulls in fish docks, and for photography from a hide, a 135-millimetre telephoto lens is useful, and can provide hours of amusement developing the necessary stalking skill. Longer focal-length lenses, up to 500 millimetres, make the job of photographing birds without a hide progressively easier, but size and weight make handling of lenses over 300 millimetres difficult and for lenses over 135 millimetres focal length a firm tripod or a rifle-butt shoulder tripod is necessary.

*Hide at a
Heron nest*

For photography at the nest (see Protection of Birds Act, page 19) a 'hide' is essential. Of much the same construction as a tent, of canvas or a similar material on a rigid but collapsable framework roughly 3 feet square and 4 or 5 feet high, the hide itself should merge with its surroundings, if necessary being disguised with local vegetation. Portable hides are also of great use in making extended close observations of birds at the nest, feeding – almost anywhere.

Many people will have experienced the value of the large permanent hides at some of the larger bird reserves, with the magnificent close-up views they allow of the birds moving about their business undisturbed. One advantage of a hide is that it does allow the use of a larger-format camera – nowadays 5×5 centimetres (2¼ inches square) is commoner than quarter plate.

It is worth bearing in mind that a great many photographs have now been taken of most of our breeding species at their nests, but very few good photographs exist of birds, even of common garden species, going about their day to day affairs. Photography at the nest may imply possible danger to the bird – if only in that a hide will reveal its location to other humans. A strict code of conduct must be observed – always putting the bird's interests first – when taking photographs at the nest. Any interfering vegetation should be *tied* back out of the way, not cut out, and carefully replaced when photography is over. Positioning the hide is vital, and a gradual approach is essential – the hide first erected a good distance from the nest (further in open country than in tree or scrub surroundings) and moved a little closer each day. On the other hand, photography of birds away from the nest or out of the breeding season has greater value, presents a greater challenge, and any birdwatcher taking up photography should be encouraged to try his hand at stalking his subjects. It is tremendous fun and teaches the photographer much about the habits of his quarry.

Spotted Redshank swimming

14

3. FIELDCRAFT

Clothing

Almost as important as the choice of suitable binoculars for bird watching is the choice of suitable clothing, and today the range of clothing available through sports shops, climbing equipment specialists and the wide network of ex-service equipment stores almost matches the availability and price range of binoculars and cameras.

There are several 'ideals' that a birdwatcher's clothing should try to match up to, perhaps the most obvious being that it should be hard-wearing. Many different materials possess this property – corduroy, whipcord, tweed, nylon, for example – but can have associated disadvantages: corduroy, although normally warm, can soak up rain to a tremendous extent, and not only become chilling but rather cumbrously heavy to wear; nylon, on the other hand, is light and waterproof, hard-wearing under normal conditions, but very prone to tearing by thorns. Silent movement is often a great advantage, and an additional problem with some plastics and oilskins is that they may rustle or crackle, especially when twigs brush across them.

In most circumstances inconspicuous clothing is to be regarded as an advantage, but always remember in mountain areas and on remote moorlands or marshes – anywhere that there is any real possibility of getting lost – one of the first rules is that at least some conspicuous piece of clothing should be worn or carried, usually socks, hat or anorak. Bright colours can be of great assistance to searchers in wide-open or rocky surroundings, and in extreme cases could mean the difference between life and death. Obviously if you are to watch birds in any remote situations where an accident – even as simple as a sprained ankle – could be troublesome or even dangerous, the normal rules of survival, such as those used by climbers, should be followed. Briefly these are that clothing and footwear should be suitable for the task; that adequate warm clothing is in reserve (a polythene 'survival bag' to maintain body heat is readily and cheaply available from outdoor equipment shops and is easily carried; and that some means of attracting search parties should be carried — normally conspicuous clothing and a whistle. Obviously maps are always useful (Ordnance Survey 1 : 50,000 and 1 : 25,000) and in really remote areas an adequate map and a compass are essential.

Generally, clothing should match the expected climatic conditions, bearing in mind that too hot can be just as unpleasant as too cold. A useful compromise can be reached with easily removed sweaters and a light but windproof and waterproof anorak. In all cases, ease of movement should not be hampered, and circulation should not be restricted by tightness at wrist or ankle as this can severely intensify the effects of cold weather. Some types of winter watching can necessitate prolonged spells with little or no movement – often lying or sitting on cold ground, so the motto is always 'be prepared'. Additional clothing can always be removed and carried in a light haversack.

Whilst showerproof clothing is often very practicable, and resists average rainfall, birdwatchers are often exposed to continuous heavy rain with little prospect of shelter. Many experienced watchers dislike the use of stormproof clothing of the oilskin type as it is heavy, awkward and noisy, and condensation inside offsets any protective value from the elements. Perhaps the best solution is an easily carried, very lightweight plastic cape or mackintosh, which is both rainproof and windproof and used only when needed.

Footwear

Much the same series of pros and cons can be applied to footwear: obviously it should be capable of the job required, without being cumbersome or over-heavy. Considering the extreme first: thigh waders are only occasionally needed and are very difficult indeed to wear, being especially tiring over long distances. Whilst their use in deep water in winter is almost unavoidable, many prefer light trousers or swimming shorts, worn with or without elderly tennis shoes, to handle wet areas in summer. The same clothing is often worn by those tackling estuary mud flats, for here tennis shoes can protect the feet against glass, sharp shells and so on.

On many summer occasions, when the going is not too ankle-twisting, heavy shoes are quite adequate, but do remember that strands of bramble or rose can be very painful when dragged across an ankle. Opinion is divided on heavier forms of footwear. Wellington boots are often more practical in muddy or wet grass conditions, but suffer from problems of condensation inside as well as weight. Heavy boots of the climbing variety are essential in some circumstances – where actual rock-climbing or heavy walking is involved – but in many cases are adequately, and more cheaply, replaced by rubber-soled fell-boots, which may provide the nearest-to-ideal bird watching footwear.

For hand covering in winter only one major point needs making: most binoculars have a centrally mounted focusing wheel which is hard to manipulate in thick gloves, and especially difficult, if not impossible, to use wearing mittens.

The approach

Having already said that in remote, exposed or dangerous areas some element of conspicuous clothing should be worn or at least carried, from the point of view of the naturalist wishing to obtain a close view of a bird, the opposite is the case. Really there are two main factors in obtaining a good view of a bird: to have the light in the right place (i.e. not looking directly into the sun), and to be inconspicuous.

Getting the best lighting conditions is obviously an art that comes with experience. In some circumstances, of course, it just is not possible and the best must be made of a bad job, but identifying birds in silhouette against the sun is difficult, and the lack of a good view is frustrating. With localities that you know, planning visits to avoid bad sun conditions is often possible, though on estuaries or at the sea getting the conditions of wind or tide right may well be more important. As birds have next to no sense of smell, no problem arises about being down-wind of the bird you are stalking, but the tears that come to the eyes when looking into a stiff, cold breeze hamper vision and reduce the enjoyment of the occasion. The birdwatcher must also make some allowances for lighting conditions – very bright light can produce quite extraordinarily misleading colours, as can the apricot flush of dawn or a really rosy sunset.

A generally quiet and cautious approach also is vital – laughter, loud talking, or sudden movements can warn birds of your approach and have them well away and out of sight before you

Shelduck

reach them. It is well worth practising the Red Indian trick of quiet movement through woodland: avoiding snapping off branches, collisions with bunches of dead leaves, and especially treading on old branches on a woodland floor which can break with a crack like gunshot. Use whatever cover may be available, a hedgerow for example, and when you reach a gateway, scan carefully before crossing. On sea-walls a good wide view can usually be obtained from the top, but if a bay is being approached, especially if it is known to be a favourite resting or feeding place for ducks, geese or waders, drop down behind the sea-wall a quarter of a mile or so beforehand, and make a cautious final approach, the last stage stomach-to-ground, before peering over the top.

These tactics come more easily with experience and before long are almost automatic. They are augmented also by any increase in knowledge of the birds under observation. Some species may be specially confiding – for example the Long-tailed Tit, which may even perch on your arms, shoulders or head should you encounter a family party, and press yourself, quite immobile, back into the hedge. Others are not so confiding and never will be, and these are birds to be particularly careful about, for their alarm calls can disturb everything within hearing. Good examples are the Blackbird, flying chattering and scolding away in garden or woodland, or the shrill alarm call of the Redshank piercing the peace of marshes or water meadows.

Anticipation also grows with experience; a visual assessment of the habitat – the types of plants, the presence of water, and so on – will tell you many of the birds to expect and allows you to approach accordingly. In much the same way that birds can hear *you* coming, you can be forewarned of *their* presence by listening for calls or song, and for many of the secretive or timid species a good working knowledge of various calls increases greatly your chances of good sighting.

Bird watching ethics

In all circumstances *the birds' interests must come first*: never harry birds or disturb them unnecessarily, especially in periods of severe weather or when the birds are newly arrived and very tired migrants. Examples here would be Fieldfares and Redwings feeding on fruit in conditions of severe frost or heavy snow, or perhaps a warbler or a Bluethroat desperately trying to feed and recover after a long migratory flight. After all, we want birds to watch in the future, and conservation is not founded on disturbance.

The law

These cautions are even more necessary when applied to nesting birds. Under the Wildlife and Countryside Act various levels of protection are afforded, especially to rarer birds during the breeding season. This is a new Act, with regional variations and still in the process of becoming established. For the latest information contact the RSPB or Nature Conservancy Council.

Licences to observe or photograph the more closely protected species can be obtained in justifiable cases through the Nature Conservancy. The following code of conduct appears in the BTO guide to the Nest Record Scheme, and is worth following: 'Each observer must exercise a sense of responsibility, always putting the birds' interests first if a visit might endanger the nest. This applies with redoubled force where rare species are involved. This section explains in fair detail how to conduct observations without putting nests at risk, and indicates things that should not be done. The potential risks may be reviewed here. Basically there are three: (a) accidentally damaging the nest; (b) causing desertion; (c) revealing a nest to predators. In practice the exercise of due care eliminates the chance of accidental damage. Desertion may arise through natural causes, such as adverse weather, food shortage or the death of a parent, as well as from human disturbance. Sometimes, too, for one of several reasons, a whole clutch fails to hatch despite being incubated well beyond the normal period; eventually the nest is abandoned, but clearly not through any immediate outside influence. With most species the great majority of nesting failures are due to predation by crows, stoats, weasels, squirrels, small rodents, cats or other predators. Observers often fear that increased predation may result from their leaving a track or scent trail to nests, but a two-year investigation of this possibility showed that nests visited frequently in bushes, hedges and thick undergrowth had a similar rate of success to others left undisturbed between laying and fledging. This finding is supported by the consistency of the results obtained when analysing different observers' records. That heavy predation occurs in the absence of human involvement may also be demonstrated by searching a new, completely undisturbed area late in the season: commonly, far more nests are found which show obvious signs of failure (e.g. sucked-out eggs) than those which show signs of successful rearing.'

Avoiding damage to known nests depends largely on common sense, but remember that nests as yet undiscovered may be highly vulnerable. Therefore take care not to dislodge any when pushing through dense scrub. In seabird colonies the risk of treading on nests or downy young is obvious but there is a similar danger when searching for other ground-nests (e.g. those of Snipe, Skylark, Willow Warbler).

While we are considering our manners so far as birds are concerned, let us not forget our fellow birdwatchers. Others may wish to see the birds, so we should not interfere with – especially not destroy – unwanted bits of the habitat. Please do not stand up and walk off when you have seen your fill, for others may be watching at the same time and will not be too pleased at the precipitate departure of both yourself *and* the bird. Sometimes it may be necessary to flush a sitting bird – with some waders, for example, the wing and tail pattern may be the major clue to identification – but if this is the case try and make sure that everyone else has had a satisfactory view beforehand.

A final point under this heading: remember that birdwatchers are very dependent on landowners' goodwill and that farmers have a living to earn. Keep to the footpaths, ask permission *first* if you wish to gain access to land (most landowners are courteous and co-operative if you explain the purpose of your visit) – in fact, always follow the Country Code:

> Guard against all risk of fire.
> Fasten all gates.
> Keep dogs under proper control.
> Keep to the paths across farmland.
> Avoid damage to fences, hedges and walls.
> Leave no litter.
> Safeguard water supplies.
> Protect wildlife, wild plants and trees.
> Go carefully on country roads.
> Respect the life of the countryside.

4. WHERE AND WHEN

The previous chapters have underlined the fact that one of the most appealing things about birds is their almost universal presence – wherever you go there will be birds to watch, interesting behaviour to study. Perhaps the most striking example of this widespread availability of birds is the book by John Buxton, who studied the Redstart in great detail during his monotonous existence as a prisoner of war in the Second World War, and wrote a fascinating book about the bird afterwards.

As the scenery and vegetation of our countryside varies from region to region with changing geology and climate, so too do the birds you can hope to see. It is difficult to see which of the two has the greater effect on bird life: perhaps the best general rule is that generally bird diversity increases as you move eastward into Europe, and decreases as you move westward towards Ireland. On a smaller scale, the number of bird species is generally dependent on the variety of habitats available – far more species will be present, for example, in a countryside of mixed arable farmland and woodland with hedgerows than there will be in an adjacent area of uniform grazing, marshland or rough heather moorland.

Just as there are specialist craftsmen and general workers in human circles, so there are specialist birds for almost every habitat and 'general purpose' birds that manage well in a considerable variety of surroundings. Books on bird biology give much fuller details of the fascinating adaptations to their

*Nightjar
at dusk*

specialised lives of birds as diverse as the Crossbill of conifer forests, the Nightjar, a woodland 'filter-feeder', and the Avocet, 'sweeping' food from the surface of East Anglian salt lagoons.

Curlew Sandpiper

Migration

Many birds migrate – that is, perform long seasonal journeys to escape severe weather or to reach more plentiful food supplies. In Britain we have a wide variety of visiting migrants – some just passing through on their way north in spring from Africa to breeding grounds near the Arctic Circle (such as the Greenland race of the Wheatear), to return southwards later in autumn. Others arrive with us in spring from Africa and stay through our insect-rich summer to breed – for example many of the warblers like the Chiffchaff and the Blackcap, together with the Swallow and the Cuckoo. Still others move south and west across Europe as winter begins, and arrive to spend the hardest period in the warmer oceanic climate of Britain – birds such as the Waxwing (plate 3) and the Fieldfare and Redwing, two beautiful thrushes that are specially plentiful on autumn hawthorn berries, and which often become very tame during prolonged cold or snowy spells. These will return north in spring to their breeding grounds, following the thawing winter snows. To a large extent these birds that breed near or even north of the Arctic Circle are rather specialised, for time is at a premium. Perhaps some of the best examples are some of the wading birds – the Knot, the Curlew Sandpiper or the Dunlin, for example. These must fly north from Africa, ready to take advantage of the prodigious quantity of insects that are produced in the Arctic during the very brief summer. Immediately the long flight is over, coinciding with the thawing ice in mid to late May, the serious business of nest-building and egg-laying must begin, for by the end of July the birds will be wanting to fly south again with their newly reared families.

A consequence of this pattern of migrants coming and going is that some of the birds of an area will change during the four seasons of the year – another element of variety. Besides this, extremes of weather can bring to Britain unusual numbers of some species normally from elsewhere in Europe, and occasionally very rare birds from great distances. Most autumns, for example, the occasional hurricane from the Caribbean will move up the eastern coast of America before crossing the North Atlantic using up the last of its terrific energy. The winds that accompany these spent hurricanes are very strong westerlies, sufficiently strong to give a tail-wind 'assisted passage' to several American visitors to our islands — each year many waders make this crossing, and, more rarely, quite small birds such as the American warblers survive the journey. On the other hand, occasionally autumn weather conditions over the continent of Europe will produce a gentle but long-lived easterly current of air from eastern Asia, and on such air-streams we may be lucky enough to see some Far Eastern birds. For example in 1968 such a period of weather produced at least eighteen Pallas Warblers (an attractive Chiffchaff-like bird from eastern Siberia, with three striking pale stripes on its head and a yellow patch on its rump, weighing perhaps only 8 or 9 grams – see plate 4) in a month or so in Britain, as many as had ever been recorded here before.

Urban birds

Perhaps we could best start this guide to 'where and when' in and around our towns and their gardens and parks. In strictly urban surroundings it may well be that the House Sparrow and Starling are the most numerous birds, but there can be few gardens that do not occasionally see Jackdaws, Blackbirds, Greenfinches and Dunnocks. Even in these circumstances a regularly stocked bird-table can be a tremendous attraction – not only will it provide much better views of the birds in the garden, but it will tempt Blue and Great Tits from some distance. With the larger gardens and greater number of open spaces in suburbia, the number of birds increases accordingly; the tits are regular visitors and may use nestboxes, Robins, Song Thrushes and occasionally Mistle Thrushes appear, and wintry weather will bring in Chaffinches and Wrens. Parks, even those in central London, can produce a great variety of species such as Mallard, Canada Goose, Mute Swan, Coot, Moorhen, and Nuthatch, with regular flocks of gulls during the winter. Tawny Owls breed successfully (sometimes in nestboxes) in Kensington Gardens. Because they are so used to people (and to being fed!) birds in parks are often good subjects for close observation, and St James's Park, with its collection of ducks and geese of many species, is a useful spot for early steps in identification.

23

Feral pigeons – the 'Trafalgar Square' type escapes from pigeon-fanciers' lofts – besides being numerous enough to be a nuisance in some buildings and railway stations may be a nuisance in the garden, keeping other more desirable birds away from any food that is put out for them. Commonly they may be joined by Woodpigeons – usually so timid in country surroundings, but bold and often very well-fed in town parks and gardens. Over much of Britain and Ireland a newcomer has joined these two – the Collared Dove, smaller and slimmer than the Woodpigeon, sandy coloured, with a small blackish half-collar on each side of the neck and with a large whitish patch on the underside of the tail. Only in the middle 1950s did the first pairs of this species breed in East Anglia and south-east England, having spread very rapidly across Europe from the area east of the Mediterranean since about 1900. This very rapid spread continued within the British Isles, and within twenty years birds were nesting on islands off the west coast of Ireland. In Tralee, way down in the south-west in County Kerry, flocks of several hundred Collared Doves are now seen, and elsewhere, in some towns in eastern England, especially in Kent, the species has reached such levels as to be regarded by some as a pest.

Collared Dove

Rural gardens

Country gardens, of course, see a far greater variety of birds, as they can draw on nearby woodland and farmland. Rooks often appear, as do other tits – Coal, Marsh, or Willow (the last two difficult to separate, a task best attempted after listening to recordings of their voices) and occasionally the Long-tailed Tit (colloquially 'Bottle Tit'). Additional charm is lent to any garden by Linnets and Goldfinches. The collective noun for a number of Goldfinches is, most appropriately, a 'charm'. Another finch, the Bullfinch, can certainly add to the charm of any garden, for it is one of our most beautiful birds. Keen gardeners, however, are far from enthusiastic as the flower-buds of Forsythia, Daphne and several fruit bushes or trees are greatly favoured by Bullfinches, especially in years when their natural foods like the seeds of ash or dock are in short supply. Nuthatches can be much more frequent visitors to the bird-table, where they may be joined by the handsome Great Spotted Woodpecker – white beneath, black above with white bars, with a scarlet patch beneath the tail and, in the male, a scarlet patch on the back of the head. A bird of rather similar situations, in that it lives much of its life on the trunks of trees, the Treecreeper visits old trees in country gardens but is not tempted by the bird-table.

Some summer visitors also will visit country gardens, and may well breed in them – warblers such as the Willow Warbler or Chiffchaff in rough grassland or brambles under trees, or the Whitethroat in the same bramble or nettle patches or in the hedges. Cuckoos also may visit these areas, and Whitethroats and Dunnocks are frequently victims of their parasitic habits.

Kestrel hovering

Farmland

Farmland, too, shares some of the garden birds we have already talked about. It does, though, have some specially characteristic ones, such as the two Partridges, Common and Red-legged. Regrettably the increasingly modern techniques of farming are reducing the food supply of the Common Partridge considerably, and this once common game bird is now becoming rather rare in some areas. The more strikingly coloured Red-legged, or French Partridge, commonest in eastern England, is holding its own rather better. Another game bird, the Pheasant, long ago imported from the Far East, is a handsome addition to our bird life, with coppery body, bottle-green head, and very long tail feathers shown off to best effect as he struts across the plough or stubble.

Even if naturalists had not already considered the Skylark as almost the emblem of English farmland, poets and songwriters certainly have. Singing cheerfully whilst hovering high over its midfield territory and nest, the Skylark is entirely characteristic of walks in the country, as it sings from early spring to late autumn (and on occasional fine warm winter days, too).

Over the fields (and sometimes over town parks, rough places or roadside verges) can occasionally be seen our commonest bird of prey, the Kestrel. The old name for this species is 'windhover', and indeed the bird is master of the art of hanging stationary in the air, watching for the movement of a vole or a mouse – or even a large beetle – sometimes a hundred feet or more below. Most predatory birds – that is those that live on other animals – are by nature equipped with exceptionally keen sight, and also often with very well developed hearing. This is especially so in the owl family, who do much of their hunting at dusk or during the night, when acute sight is of less value. Since the very cold winter of 1962–3 the most frequent farmland owl, the very pale, white below, sandy above Barn Owl has become far less common than it was, but now at long last there are some signs of a recovery. As its name implies it nests in farm buildings, especially deserted or semi-ruined ones. Fortunately it is generally looked on with favour by the farmer, as it contributes to the balance of nature by taking a proportion of rats and house mice among its prey. The Little Owl, with characteristic yelping call, is another farmland bird as well as a woodland one. A smaller bird, streaked grey brown with white spots, it lacks the heart-shaped face of the Barn Owl and features far more insects in its diet. Despite its size – it stands at 8 or 9 inches – it will tackle and kill birds as big as Blackbirds – or even Mistle Thrushes – to feed its young, which are normally reared in a hollow in a tree.

Hedgerows are most valuable to bird populations on farmland, as they provide a place to nest and a source of both food and shelter at all times of the year. The birds that use them are much the same as in gardens – Blackbirds, Thrushes, Robins, Wrens and Dunnocks for example, but in areas of arable or cereal farming species like the handsome Yellowhammer (whose song is often described, rather hopefully, as 'a little bit of bread and no cheese') with bold yellow and black head, or the very drab buff

Corn Bunting

26

Corn Bunting, whose song most resembles the jangling of a bunch of keys, may be seen. Of the summer visitors the White-throat probably is the most characteristic, but even this bird has become scarce in some areas since the winter of 1968–9, when a mysterious fate – still unexplained – overtook the majority of the population either in the wintering areas of Africa or on the way there or back. At the time of writing, the rate of recovery is rather slow. All in all, because of the regular layout of the land, the rotation of crops and the types of birds present, farmland presents one of the best areas for some of the studies described in the next chapter.

During the autumn and winter months, some large flocks of birds gather on the fields. Often these are House and Tree Sparrows, Linnets, Chaffinches, Greenfinches, Yellowhammers or Skylarks feeding on weed seeds left after crop harvesting, but also large flocks of Rooks and Jackdaws, Lapwing and gulls gather to feed on worms, insect larvae, or just to rest. Gulls are now so much a feature of our inland countryside, following the plough to gather worms from freshly overturned clods (Black-headed Gull), or feeding widely scattered across meadows (Common Gull), that it is difficult to think that this habit in so-called 'sea' gulls has only developed since the early years of this century, when the Black-headed Gull – now one of the 'regulars' of town parks and lakes – was a great rarity in London.

Woodland

Many of the birds of gardens and farmland that we have been considering are basically woodland species, and are still to be met with commonly on woodland walks. The type of woodland, though, makes a very considerable difference, and most of the species already discussed are associated with broad-leaved, or deciduous, woodland consisting mainly of trees such as oak, elm, ash, beech, birch and sycamore. These woodlands tend to have a fair amount of undergrowth – bramble, hawthorn, elder and so on, mixed with plenty of herbaceous plants – which provides good feeding and nesting areas for the population of small birds. It stands to reason that the amount of insect and plant food available is greater in this sort of wood than it would be in an area with little or no undergrowth, and this is the main reason that deciduous woodland normally holds so many more birds than mature stands of conifer. Where conifers, sometimes pine but more often spruce or other imported trees, are grown commercially they are planted close together to encourage rapid growth and straight trunks with few side branches. The close growth cuts down the light penetration, and side branches do not develop, but neither does any undergrowth. Together with this, the 'seeds' of conifers are only available to a few specialist species like the Crossbill, whose scissor-like overlapping beak can reach between the segments of the cones. Crossbills are rare birds, and some mature areas of conifer do not contain much more than Goldcrests, Chaffinches, Coal Tits and Woodpigeons.

However, the first ten to fifteen years after the planting of conifers produces a really rich area: the trees are not tall enough to shade out smaller plants, food abounds, and shelter is plentiful as the trees are planted so close. Thus the despair with which many country-lovers, as well as birdwatchers, greet the new plantation should always be tempered with an eager expectation of the benefits of the first few years, and with the knowledge that the 'black canyon' conditions will not last for ever, as commercial forestry blocks will be regularly felled for timber and subsequently replanted. At the moment one or two scarce species are benefiting greatly from such newly planted blocks; the Sparrowhawk is increasing now in the west and north after the disastrous 1960s when the effects of the ravages of poisoning by agrochemicals were most felt.

There are some species, like the Tree Pipit and the Nightjar, that we expect to find in areas of freshly cleared land and during the first couple of years after the new planting. Other scrubland species soon begin to appear, becoming more common as time goes by – Linnets, Goldfinches, Bullfinches, Blackbirds, Wrens, Dunnocks and Whitethroats are a few examples. As the cover begins to develop, one or two more interesting, and perhaps slightly unexpected species begin to appear: the skulking but very handsome Lesser Whitethroat (which has a song rather similar to the Yellowhammer, but without the 'cheese'), and the Reed Bunting and Grasshopper Warbler – both birds more often associated with rather wetter areas. In the remoter areas of the west and north, you may be lucky enough to see a hunting Hen Harrier, regularly patrolling its beat on rather stiff wings, or, at dusk, a Long-eared Owl looking for roosting birds or foraging field mice or voles.

More mature deciduous woodland, especially beech or oak, usually has some of the other owls – in some parts the Little Owl is commonest, in others the Tawny holds sway. The Tawny Owl is the 'too-whit-too-whoooo' owl – the Little Owl has a puppy-like yelp or a high-pitched 'poo-oop'. In some parts of the country Long-eared Owls either spend the winter or breed in both coniferous and deciduous woods. These owls have long and always conspicuous tufts of feathers over the eyes – the so-called 'ears'. They are rather quiet, hunt normally only at dusk or after, and being generally inconspicuous are probably rather commoner and more widespread than we think.

HEN HARRIER   R.A.R.

Quartering Hen Harrier

Long-eared Owls hunting through the roosting bushes and Sparrowhawks taking old and young birds alike are just two of the ever-present threats faced by small bird populations in woodland. A pair of Sparrowhawks and their young may take between 2,500 and 5,000 Chaffinch-sized birds a year as food. There is some reason to suppose that a proportion of those taken are the slower, possibly less alert, and often sick individuals – and here the predator does a useful job in removing such undesirable specimens from the population. The others, of course, can be well spared, as the whole woodland pattern is in balance: generally rather more young of most small birds than are needed are produced, and this predation is just one of the natural ways in which the balance is maintained. In closer view, it is most unlikely that a predator would ever seriously threaten its prey species in natural circumstances – if it did, what would there be left for it to live on? Figures like those above do give some idea of the productivity of small birds, though. In some middling-sized counties there may be two hundred or more pairs of Sparrowhawks, so 600,000 or so small birds may be needed to feed them each year. It is somewhat surprising to discover that his can indeed be done – easily, and without any dramatic declines in species like the Chaffinch! Over and over again we come upon these instances of the flexibility in the natural scheme of things, the ability of the birds to redress any change in balance. Only when man makes sweeping changes do troubles normally arise, and these usually compare in size to natural disasters such as the 1962–3 hard winter, which killed, for example, roughly seventy per cent of our Wrens.

During the breeding season, losses may be even higher if robbed nests are included; woodland birds such as the Magpie (also common on farmland) and Jay take many eggs and young, as do some mammals like squirrels, stoats and weasels, and sometimes even field mice. It comes as a surprise to most nest-recorders (see Chapter 5) that so many of the nests whose progress they are recording fail for one reason or another. This is yet another example of the great reproductive flexibility of birds.

Old woodland – especially deciduous – takes on additional character of its own once branches start to break off, timber to soften and rot, trees to fall – all providing new 'niches' for additional species to exploit. Elderly timber in woodland that is not managed with the hygiene unfortunately so popular with commercial foresters, shelters much more insect life, and falling trees leave gaps in the canopy so that patches of undergrowth can develop more. Holes can be cut in such trees by woodpeckers anxious to nest or to remove the grubs of boring insects; these nest holes, used once or twice by the woodpeckers, are then used by a variety of other species. The Green Woodpecker is as much a bird of park or farmland as of woods, as its main food is ants. It seems that with the loss of so much permanent grassland there are generally fewer ants in Britain than before the Second World War, and Green Woodpeckers are only very slowly recovering from the effects of the cold winter of 1962–3. The two Spotted Woodpeckers – Greater and Lesser – did not suffer so severely. The Great Spotted is quite common in many areas, and regularly visits country garden bird-tables. The Lesser Spotted is a much less conspicuous bird, as well as being considerably smaller

(Chaffinch-size), and is often considered to be rare. Perhaps this also is an overlooked species, and at the present moment there are signs of increases in numbers in several parts of the country generally associated with outbreaks of Dutch Elm disease. Species 'following on' in woodpecker holes include Jackdaws, a great many Starlings, and many of our tits – the commonest users being Great Tits and Blue Tits. Only one tit regularly digs its own nest hole – the Willow Tit – and this usually in soft rotten timber. Its near relative, the Marsh Tit, uses old woodpecker holes, natural crevices and so on. The two are generally regarded as difficult to separate: very similar in plumage, the Willow Tit has a rather thicker-set neck and a pale buffish patch on the otherwise brown feathers of the closed wing, but the best way to distinguish them is by the call – the Marsh Tit a strident 'pitch-you' and the Willow Tit a rather diffident 'dee, dee, dee'. In conifers the Coal Tit, with a white patch on the back of its head, is generally the most frequent, but in some areas of Scotland, especially in the Cairngorm Mountain region, the exciting and handsome Crested Tit is often quite numerous.

Lesser Spotted Woodpecker

Mountain and moorland

Talking of Crested Tits leads us on to look at some of the birds of mountain and moorland. Speyside, in Inverness-shire, the home of much of our Crested Tit population, is now renowned as the centre of the revival of our Osprey population – here, near the

31

Golden Eagle

home many years ago of the last pair of Ospreys to breed before egg collectors drove them away, several pairs now breed each year. Initially very strict secrecy was necessary, and after the news was released of their presence, strict protective measures including barbed wire and electronic alarm systems came into force. Even so, collectors are still active, and several clutches of eggs have been taken. These splendid birds — fish-eaters the size of a small eagle — can now be easily seen from the undisturbing concealment of a hide.

The Golden Eagle, monarch of our birds of prey and our only native eagle, is unfortunately much more difficult to see. Apart from a pair in Lakeland, the population is thinly spread mostly in the remote mountain areas of western Scotland and the western isles, and has suffered very severely in the last few years. Regrettably there remains considerable pressure on the population from those who think that an eggshell locked in a cabinet (secretly, for collection is now illegal) is more satisfactory than an eagle soaring freely over a highland glen. Add to this the furtive pressures – the mysterious shootings, broken eggs or nest fires perhaps caused by gamekeepers who feel that the eagles may be taking too many grouse from the moors or disturbing the autumn shooting of their masters! In the last few decades an additional threat has appeared: even in the remotest parts of Scotland, considerable traces of some of the chemicals used on farmland, and especially in sheep dips, have appeared in Golden Eagles and their eggs, reducing very considerably the fertility of the birds and the number of eaglets successfully produced each year.

32

1. Pectoral and Semipalmated Sandpipers: a most unusual photograph of these two vagrant American waders together on this side of the Atlantic.

2. Herring Gull, victim of an oil-leak from a tanker.

3. Waxwing, an occasional wanderer to Britain from Europe, in 'irruption' years often feeding on garden berries.

4. Pallas Warbler, a tiny and very rare visitor from Asia.

5. Phragmites reed beds, beloved of warblers and Bearded Tits, and often used by many species for autumn roosts.

6. Great Crested Grebe and chicks 'riding pillion'. This species survived the threats of fashion to fall foul of water pollution.

7. A Shelduck 'parliament' — an early-morning display gathering.

8. The drake Pintail is one of our most immaculately beautiful ducks.

9. Greylag Geese in flight: note how conspicuous the pale forewing is.

10. Black-tailed Godwits taking off at the tide edge, showing well the very long bill and the bold black and white wing pattern, a good identification characteristic.

11. Gannets on Grassholm. The chicks (foreground) used to be taken for food on many remote islands. In the background a mass of sitting adults can be seen, each two beak-thrust distances from its neighbour!

12. A Guillemot colony on the cliffs, many of the adults with quite well-grown young, nearly ready to leave.

The Peregrine Falcon shows a similar alarming decrease – of about 800 territories occupied in the 1930s, only thirty per cent were occupied in 1963, and only ten per cent produced young. A bird of coastal and mountain cliffs and precipices, the Peregrine was once reasonably common in southern England, and not too long ago, but it is now restricted to the remoter areas of the north and west. The picture is the same as for the Golden Eagle: most predatory birds are at the top of a food-chain – that is they eat a number of birds or other animals that, in their turn, have eaten other smaller animals that have eaten animals or plants contaminated with pesticide residues. These residues are so persistent (their life is measured in tens of years) that they may pass unchanged from stage to stage up the chain. Whilst in nature things are not so greatly simplified as this, a mechanism of multiplication in a food-chain is apparent, and in the long-lived birds at the end of most food-chains, it is not surprising to find lethal, or at least near-lethal, doses of some agrochemical residues. The latest score is heartening. With the outlawing of lethal pesticides, Peregrine and eagle numbers have recovered surprisingly rapidly.

Characteristic moorland birds often forming the main food items for birds like the Peregrine (female Peregrines will sometimes tackle wild geese) and Merlin (a smaller falcon with similar habits) include the Golden Plover and the Ring Ouzel, whose song (rather Mistle-Thrush-like) is another characteristic of wild rocky glens and gorges on the mountain side. The Ring Ouzel is the mountain equivalent of the Blackbird, the male slatey grey rather than black, with a white crescentic 'bib'. Other small birds typical of moorland are Twite (the mountain equivalent of the Linnet), Stonechat, Whinchat and Wheatear, the last three amongst the most colourful and beautiful of the smaller members of the thrush family. Both Stonechats and Whinchats are birds of coastal areas also, and are frequently seen perched atop a sprig of gorse, flicking wings and tail and 'chack-ing' approaching intruders. Further north in Scotland, we are often left with only one fairly common species of small bird – the Meadow Pipit – drab and streaked – but absolutely typical of the areas and often the birdwatcher's only companion away from birch scrub or water in these areas.

The wetter regions of moorland will often hold Curlew, with the well-known descending bubbling trill used in song flights to outline the margins of its territory. The very much smaller Dunlin, better known as an estuary bird in winter, also breeds in this type of locality amongst the bog cotton, but the Greenshank, in size between the two, and a scarce breeding bird, normally chooses rather dryer ground. One of our rarest breeding birds has the most select breeding ground imaginable – the tops of our highest peaks. Thus the Dotterel – another wader – is restricted to a few areas like the Cairngorms, and is made no easier to find by its extreme tameness. It is one of the few birds in which the male is more drably plumaged than the female and does much of the hard work in rearing the family, including incubating the eggs. Often sitting birds are so determined that they will allow themselves to be stroked on the nest. Similarly tame is the Ptarmigan – feathery-footed to walk on the snow of its mountain-top home.

Ptarmigan

Water birds

Mountain or moorland lakes in the far north-west hold another exciting family of birds, the divers. Both Red-throated and Black-throated Divers breed regularly, and the larger Great Northern, made famous by Arthur Ransome, does so occasionally. These three species are amongst the most spectacularly handsome of British birds – remarkably in that two, the Great Northern and the Black-throated, are combinations of only black, grey and white. The 'song' too, is remarkable. The Americans call the family the loons, because of the similarity of their voice to uncontrolled maniacal laughter – it is truly one of the sounds of north-western Scotland – eerie, but very wild and thoroughly typical of remoteness.

These lakes run down to the sea often as fast-moving streams, full of salmon and trout, which are beloved not only by fly fishermen but by two of the 'sawbill' ducks – adapted for fish feeding by having serrated edges to their beaks – the Goosander and the Red-breasted Merganser. Despite oppressive measures, both are currently extending their ranges. Two small birds also characterise such fast-moving mountain streams, the Grey Wagtail (a bird of waterfall, weir and mill-race in the south) and the Dipper. The last, a relative of the thrushes, is a most interesting bird as it feeds underwater. Often a view from a bridge will allow you to look down on a Dipper, walking without difficulty along the river bed in 18 inches or so of water, searching for insect larvae. They hop quite unconcerned into the water, and may swim in search of food in water several feet deep using their wings in underwater slow-motion 'flight', before bobbing up again and perching, tail cocked like a large Wren, white belly prominent, on a favourite boulder.

Areas of fresh water, many of them nowadays artificial in origin but very welcome now so much natural marshland has been drained, provide some of the richest year-round bird watching available over much of Britain. Urban and industrial development, with consequent demands on clay, sand and ballast for bricks, cement and concrete, has caused the formation of chains of artificially flooded areas in river valleys, and these have been augmented by reservoirs built to satisfy our ever-increasing demands for water. Although many of these 'bonus' bird habitats are now under very serious pressure from other forms of human recreational activity (power boating and water-skiing being the most damaging) a large number still remain, used for fishing, derelict and overgrown, or used for water storage, on which birds can live unmolested.

A change in our attitude to the wearing of bird feathers, coupled with this increase in suitable waters, led to a great recovery in the much reduced Great Crested Grebe population around the turn of the century, and these beautiful birds (plate 6) can now be seen over much of the British Isles. Look for them particularly in the spring, when their fascinating courtship 'dance' on the surface of the water can be closely watched. Common on big waters, small lakes and marshland ditches alike is the Little Grebe or Dabchick, a smaller relative of the Great

Dipper

Goosander

Crested Grebe. On some larger and deeper water areas, including some of the reservoirs near London, as well as on our estuaries, you may be lucky enough to see during the winter one of the rarer grebes which usually breed further north – the Red-necked, the Black-necked, or the Slavonian. The last two in winter plumage present a problem in identification, as the upturned beak of the Black-necked Grebe (perhaps the best field character) can only be seen in a good close-up view.

In much the same situations as the rarer grebes in winter – large reservoirs – can be seen the two sawbills already mentioned, the Goosander and Red-breasted Merganser. Most years they are joined by small numbers of a third sawbill – the Smew from Arctic Russia. This is probably one of our most beautiful ducks – the male white and grey, with black-line markings, the female grey and white, with a reddish-brown head. During the winter months many normally estuarine ducks may be found well inland on freshwater areas – 'dabbling' ducks (those that feed by up-ending in shallow water) like Mallard, Wigeon, Teal, Shoveller and Pintail, or the usually smaller, rather dumpy 'diving' ducks which dive, often deeply, in search of food, like the neat black and white Tufted Duck and the Pochard.

The Mute Swan, especially stately with wings raised in defence of its territory or young in the summer, occurs on waters of all shapes and sizes all over Britain, and is now often joined by the Canada Goose, imported by wildfowlers but now spurned by them, which is flourishing in many areas. Both of these birds can be rather harsh on the young of other water birds such as the ducks, and Moorhens and Coot. The last is a bird often present in very large numbers on big expanses of water, while only a few pairs would be found on a normal-sized lake. The Moorhen, on the other hand, is much less choosy, nesting on marshland ditches and on many quite tiny village ponds.

Many older-established inland waters are accompanied by

areas of marshy vegetation, and often by extensive reed-beds (plate 5). In autumn these may be used as a roosting site by Starlings, Sand Martins, Yellow or Pied Wagtails, but in summer they are the main breeding area for several attractive small birds. The Reed Bunting, the male with bold black cap, is almost universal and the Sedge Warbler, with strident chattering song, is also widely distributed. In southern England, the Reed Warbler, whose song is rather like that of the Sedge Warbler but perhaps more musical, and whose plumage lacks the Sedge Warbler's streaks, attaches its basket-like nest to the reed-stems, and the weaving is strong enough even to support the weight of a Cuckoo chick, for the Reed Warbler is a species frequently cuckolded. In some areas the Bittern breeds – a relative of the Heron, not frequently seen but more often heard 'booming', a distant, foghorn-like sound – and in others (especially in the South-east) the beautiful specialist Bearded Tit, which is not a real tit, but whose male has handsome black moustaches set against a dove-grey head, breeds and can be seen perching, long-tailed, on *Phragmites* stems uttering its characteristic 'ping' call. Less attractive, but equally characteristic, is the squealing cry of the skulking Water Rail.

Water Rail

Waders

In late summer muddy edges may be exposed on many fresh-water areas, and it is always worthwhile to scan the new 'shore-line' for visiting waders on return passage from their breeding grounds. In many towns sewage disposal is still by largely non-chemical means, and research work to discover any nearby sewage farms is always worthwhile. In these farms treated sewage is allowed to settle in sludge beds, and surplus treated liquids are often spread on a nearby field. Both these processes produce extensive areas (often, of course, well inland) with expanses of food-rich mud or shallow pools with lush grassy surroundings much loved by the long-beaked Snipe and, later in the year, by Teal. Many of the so-called 'marsh' waders — Sandpipers, for example — have established regular spring and autumn migration routes, passing through inland sewage farms, ballast pits or reservoirs. Some of these — the Common, Green and Wood Sandpipers, Little Stint and Ruff — are not too common elsewhere, so that a visit or series of visits, especially in autumn, may be very well worthwhile. Additionally many of the birds are naturally easily approachable, and the surroundings often offer enough cover to allow very good views indeed.

Occasionally, too, there is the chance of a really rare bird like the extraordinary Black-winged Stilt from southern Europe, which has, as its name suggests, immensely long pink legs, or a wanderer from North America like the Pectoral Sandpiper or one of the even rarer 'peeps'. These vagrants, often storm-driven, present a great challenge to identification, and special care must be taken with field notes and sketches so that there is a good chance of confirming the record. Besides the pleasures of seeing relatively tame waders (breeding in the Arctic and wintering in Africa they have little experience of mankind) sewage farms offer good chances of seeing many commoner small birds because they are relatively rich in food and are undisturbed.

The alternative area to visit to see waders, as well as ducks, geese, gulls and other seabirds, is the nearest estuary. Here the birds are in much greater numbers, in wilder and more open surroundings and consequently are by no means as approachable as they are on a small inland pool.

This point should be borne in mind by beginners, as problems of identification will be considerable in some circumstances, but to beginner and expert alike the sheer pleasure of seeing a huge flock, perhaps thousands, of Knot or Dunlin wheeling and turning in close formation against the sky takes a lot of beating. In the distance wader flocks performing these aerial evolutions look like wisps of smoke: closer to, when every bird turns as one, the flock changes colour instantly, from grey backs one second to white fronts the next – a sight very well worth watching.

Estuary birds

The very word estuary conjures up images of beautifully remote and wild places, and on some of our coasts this remains the case. Even where industrialisation is spreading across the estuaries –

factories, docks, oil refineries – there still remain extensive areas of mud or sandflat, and behind the sea-wall a great acreage of the marsh grassland favoured by Wigeon and White-fronted Geese.

Wigeon

A visit to an estuarine area requires a certain amount of planning – and often reconnoitring visits are well worthwhile. Generally, estuaries are 'winter' spots, but if winter begins in late July with the first returning passage migrants, and doesn't end until May, when the last of the northbound Sanderling and Ringed Plover have passed through, we should not complain about restricted viewing! At low tide most birds will be feeding, often a long distance from the sea-wall and widely scattered; at high tide almost all waders will be concentrated in a few roosting spots, and many of the ducks will be out in mid-stream. Thus we have a decision to make – where, and at what time, can we see the birds best. Again fieldcraft plays its part as far as sun and wind are concerned, but experience of the area is the best judge. It is difficult to produce generalised rules, but the following hints may help to increase your enjoyment: on a rising tide, station yourself, reasonably concealed, near a roosting place to watch the birds gather and the aerial evolutions as they do so (but be careful, if you must leave, not to disturb the roost – for the birds' sake as well as other birdwatchers). On a falling tide, not long after it has turned, you are likely to get the best views; both ducks and waders are keen to feed, after roosting over high water, on freshly exposed plants and animals on the mud, and are closer to the shore and perhaps just a little more tolerant of observation.

Now, what of the other birds in these areas: the creeks and fleets of the marshes may hold Dabchicks and Moorhens along with ducks like Shoveller and Teal – both of which will remain to breed in some areas. Other ducks like Wigeon and Pintail (plate 8) will commute between grassland and the mud of the estuary proper, whilst species like the Shelduck (plate 7) and further north, the Eider (the female produces down for the nest lining, which in Iceland is harvested for eiderdown and sleeping-bag use) are more strictly confined to the estuary. Also in the north huge flocks of Scaup winter as in the Firth of Forth near Edinburgh, and a few Long-tailed Ducks – rare winter visitors in the south – can be found in many Scottish estuaries. Brent Geese (plate 18), our darkest and smallest geese, are specialist feeders living mainly on a plant called *Zostera*, and occur in many estuarine areas in the south-east of England and in Ireland (a different, pale-bellied subspecies here). The other black goose, the Barnacle (separated by its silver-grey black and white face from the Brent) is really common only on the merse of the Solway, between Cumberland and Dumfries, in Ireland and on some of the Western Isles of Scotland, but odd flocks or individuals occur from time to time elsewhere.

The other geese are more grassland feeders; the White-fronted Goose is mainly a coastal marshland bird, and is occasionally joined in England by the scarcer Pink-footed and Bean Geese. Bean Geese are also scarce in Scotland, but their smaller relative the Pinkfoot is often very numerous there, not only on estuaries and marshes but in many inland and upland agricultural areas, where they feed on stubbles or potato fields. In Scotland the Greylag (plate 9), our largest native goose and the ancestor of our farmyard birds, is also widespread both on estuarine marshes and on farmland, but in England genuinely wild birds are typically estuarine and rather scarce. Here the situation is confused as Greylags have been introduced, captive, to some ornamental waters and have since escaped and established semi-wild ('feral') populations – much the same situation as for the Canada Goose imported from North America.

It is probably for their waders that estuaries are most renowned, and the many estuarine birds show a fascinating range of feeding adaptations, from the long beaks of the Curlew, curved to fit curved worm burrows, and the Godwits (plate 10), through middle-length beaks (for example, Oystercatcher or Redshank), to the short-beaked species like the Sanderling, Ringed Plover or Turnstone. These are discussed more fully in books on bird biology and feeding adaptation but it is easy to see them at work – a Godwit probing really deeply in soft mud, an Oystercatcher slicing or chiselling its way into a shellfish like a cockle, a Sanderling picking small crustaceans off the mud surface, or the Turnstone using its short, rather stout beak to overturn stones or seaweed fronds to reveal various small creatures which it can then catch and eat.

Turnstone

Seabirds

Many birdwatchers tend not to look too closely at gulls – partly because there are relatively few species, but perhaps more because they are now so usual that we take them for granted. Gulls are, however, very important – their very numbers make them so in the demands they make on available food and nesting sites (plate 17), as well as their predatory habits on the young and eggs of other species. This is particularly important so far as some of the cliff-nesting sea-birds like auks are concerned, for they are already seriously threatened by the effects of man on their environment – the discharge, accidental or deliberate, of oil into the sea and its tragic aftermath, for example.

Although some seabirds may be found on almost all parts of the coast during the breeding season, it is to the rocky islands and tall cliffs of the west and north coasts that the birdwatcher should go to see them at their best. It is now very much a question of *should* go, for modern pressures are reducing the numbers of some seabirds appreciably each year, and much of the splendour of the spectacle of a seabird colony is due to the sheer number of birds involved. Even a gull colony produces this mass effect, but to see a rocky island like Grassholm (plate 11), Ailsa Craig or Bass Rock white with thousands of Gannets, and to see the air around full of further thousands of these five-foot wingspan birds is impressive indeed, as is both the noise and the smell should you be lucky enough to visit one of the islands. Other delightful and fascinating birds abound: the Guillemots (plate 12), packed tight like rows of milk bottles on tenement doorsteps as they brood their eggs, which are pear-shaped so that they do not roll off the cliffs when accidentally kicked, on improbably narrow ledges. They are noisy birds, their garrulous and rather raucous cooing clashing with their rather peaceful aspect. Every so often on the ledges a 'bridled' Guillemot can be seen, with a white line of feathers outlining the eye and stretching back on the head like a pair of spectacles. Relatively uncommon in the south, the proportion of bridled Guillemots increases in more northerly colonies, until in Iceland and further north they may outnumber the normal form. They are not, as was once thought, a separate species but just a plumage form of the Common Guillemot, and the precise factors governing the ratio of the two types are not well understood.

Commoner amongst the tumbled boulders at the top of the cliffs, or in boulder screes, and by no means such a docile bird as the Guillemot, the Razorbill (plate 13) tends to nest in cavities, out of which its throaty rumble warns of the appropriate nature of its name. Whereas most Guillemots (except in northern Scotland) are chocolate brown and white, the Razorbill is immaculately jet-black and white, with a deeper, more savage-looking bill – a miniature Great Auk in fact.

Perhaps the most popular – and justly so – of all seabirds is the Puffin – again black and white, rather portly, with a white face patch, a permanently quizzical look and a huge, colourful parrot-shaped beak and orange legs. Confiding and inquisitive birds, their tameness is a great part of the fascination they exert over birdwatchers as they stand at the entrances to their burrows in the grassy slopes at the top of the cliffs (plate 14) or whirr around on stiff, short wings with a beakful of fish for their youngster. None of the auks appear as particularly expert fliers, and to watch Puffins in a strong crosswind making approach run after approach run in order to land near their burrow is quite fascinating – just as is watching them land on the sea. The tech-

Puffins

nique used then is simple – when they get near the surface, they stop flying and land with a considerable splash, but soon bob up perky as ever.

The Puffin seems to be suffering very severe pressures at the moment. Even on the remote island of St Kilda in the Outer Hebrides, where in the old days Puffins were hunted for food, the population has fallen from a once estimated three million pairs to only a couple of hundred thousand pairs in the space of less than ten years. As yet no reason for this decline can be found. The population has since been stable for some years.

If none of the auks are good fliers, they are expert swimmers. Although not modified to as great an extent as those of the penguins (see page 68) the wings are far more suited to propelling the birds under water than through the air. Here of course they hunt their food, which reveals further fascinating aspects of their biology: both Razorbills and Puffins feed on small fish or fry, and normally catch several before returning to their hungry chick (plate 29). The catch (often of fifteen to twenty fish) is held crosswise in the beak, alternately head to tail. How those already caught are not dropped for each new capture is only partly understood – both the jaw mechanism and the beak edges are adapted to keep a grip on several fish without severing any, but it is difficult to see how the snap and grab at a new victim can be efficiently carried out without dropping the lot!

On seabird islands or cliffs the gentle Kittiwake nests – its colonies glued on to sometimes quite tiny projections or under overhangs in situations that no other species can conquer. Kittiwakes are very noisy indeed – the call is precisely their name, the last syllable drawn out - but the chicks, with such precarious nests, have evolved a pattern of 'good behaviour' with very restricted movements alien to most gulls. Another noisy species – not really a seabird at all, but now largely restricted to seabird areas – is the Chough: with jet-black plumage that offsets well its red legs and bill, this member of the crow family is common only in parts of Wales and western Ireland.

A few other species should be mentioned – in the north, two skuas breed: both Great (plate 15) and Arctic Skuas are parasitic

Arctic Skua pursuing tern

on other birds. Their piratical attacks, often in pairs, on gulls, terns, Kittiwakes and, with the Great Skua, even on Gannets, force these unfortunate birds to drop any food they are carrying, which the skuas then eat. Remoter islands often harbour very large colonies of some truly oceanic birds, which spend most of their lives at sea, usually out of sight of land for much of the year, coming ashore only to breed and then making landfall only after dark to avoid predatory gulls – species such as the Manx Shearwater or the Storm Petrel. In passing we have discussed Gannets, and we should link them with Fulmars, as these are two seabird species that seem to be thriving at the moment – increasing in numbers steadily, perhaps benefiting more than others from the 'fish-finger age', when many fishermen gut their catch at sea, and the Fulmar is the first to be alongside to reap the rich rewards.

Observatories and sea-watching

At many points, especially headlands, around our coast in autumn and during the winter, movements – often of gigantic proportions – of seabirds can be watched. Not only do these involve our own breeding species, but others from further north – divers, grebes, Pomarine Skuas, Scoter, some of the rarer shearwaters like Sooty, Great or Cory's, Little and Sabine's Gulls, Little Auks and so on. Normally the bulk of this movement may pass out of sight of land, but in stormy weather birds on passage may pass close in and give exceptionally good views. This point on weather is always worth remembering: experience will show you the best times and places to watch and a local bird report can here be very helpful. In the west, wader spots also should be watched well after strong westerlies – perhaps the tail end of a hurricane, as American birds may have come over with these high tail winds!

The map shows the locations of the bird observatories around our coasts; the addresses of the booking secretaries can be found listed at the end of this chapter.

Most of the observatories are regarded as places for the best observation of migrants, especially in autumn, when sometimes huge 'falls' of small warblers or thrushes can occur, when every bush heaves with birds. Many of them also have a good reputation as spots where seabird movements can be observed, and some, like Skokholm, are indeed seabird colonies where a midsummer visit is amply repaid by views of the colonies. A few island observatories like Fair Isle, are positioned so that they attract weather-driven vagrants from far away – even eastern Asia – and are renowned for an astonishing proportion of very rare birds.

Nature reserves

The use of nature reserves is an admirable introduction to bird watching; often viewpoints are specially positioned, and hides erected, to let you get the best view possible of the birds. Many are chosen because of the concentration of birds of a particular sort to be found there, and often these are species not often seen elsewhere. Additional help for beginners is provided so far as ducks, geese and swans are concerned by the network of collections maintained by the Wildfowl Trust. The best-known of these is at Slimbridge, in Gloucestershire, where the birds in captivity are often joined by large numbers of wild ones, as the area is one of the major wintering areas for White-fronted Geese and Bewick's Swans (plate 16). A winter visit is good for geese and swans, and in early spring the ducks can be seen at their best, displaying in courtship – some of them with the most elaborate ceremonial. Later in the summer the many problems of identifying drakes in eclipse or moult plumage can be sorted out more easily than in the wild.

Most of the nature reserves suitable for bird watching are owned or managed by the National Trust, the Nature Conservancy or the Royal Society for the Protection of Birds, and those organisations must be consulted for full details and to obtain permits to visit (see Chapter 6). Another series of reserves is owned by the network of County Naturalists' Trusts, and more information on them can be obtained from the Society for the Promotion of Nature Reserves.

One of the principles of reserve management is that the number of visitors must be kept within reasonable proportions, and another is that visitors must conform to instructions as to where they may or may not go. These instructions may vary with the time of year – for example to avoid disturbance of shy breeding birds – but are always to be strictly obeyed as they are designed to protect the birds' interests and enhance the value of the reserve.

Much of this indicates the value of experience both in finding birds and in identifying them; to the latter there is no short cut. Very often the best way can be to join a local or county society, and to take advantage of their field meetings, where local experts are usually present to assist you. These meetings can also introduce new areas to you, but once some degree of skill in identification has been acquired, it is worth remembering that a series of visits to the same area right through the year can be far more interesting than a hotch-potch. In this way the changing pattern of the seasons can be followed, and the way the environment is used by the various species studied.

Two very useful books have been produced outlining the best bird watching spots, how to get there and, *especially important*,

1 Fair Isle   6 Sandwich Bay   11 Bardsey
2 Isle of May   7 Dungeness   12 Calf of Man
3 Spurn Point   8 Portland   13 Walney
4 Gibraltar Point 9 Lundy   14 Copeland
5 Holme   10 Cape Clear

Bird observatories in the British Isles

how and where to obtain permission before visiting privately owned or reserved areas. These are both by John Gooders: *Where to Watch Birds*, and *Where to Watch Birds in Europe*. They serve, as do conducted outings, to introduce birdwatchers to new areas, giving hints on what to see as well as where. The second volume is especially valuable now that so many of us visit other European countries either on holiday or on business. Guides to some of their reserves are produced by The Nature Conservancy, the RSPB and some of the county trusts.

All observatories are administered by independent committees. Details of those in operation, their seasons, accommodation, etc. can be obtained from the Ringing Office, British Trust for Ornithology, Beech Grove, Tring, Hertfordshire, enclosing a stamped, self-addressed envelope.

Herons

13. A Razorbill has a good wing-stretch and shake to rearrange its feathers on returning to the cliffs from the sea.

14. An evening gathering of Puffins. In the foreground one can be seen about to enter its nesting burrow.

15. *The bold white wing-flashes of the great Skua, or Bonxie, coupled with its dark plumage and size (about the same as a Great Blackbacked Gull) make this a relatively easy 'spot' when sea-watching.*

16. *Whooper Swans in Dumfries-shire — regrettably the wild trumpeting call cannot be properly conveyed in a photograph.*

17. Nesting Herring Gull — by sheer weight of numbers, these birds can be a problem amongst other seabirds. They are also a hazard to low-flying aircraft, and to public health because of their habit of feeding on refuse tips and bathing on reservoirs.

18. Dark-bellied Brent Geese feeding on Zostera, a rare marine grass.

19. Siskin and Greenfinch on a nut-bag. Only recently have Siskins started feeding in suburban gardens late in the winter, perhaps fattening up for the northward journey to the breeding grounds.

20. A close-up of the special pliers used to apply a bird ring to a Chaffinch. The rings weigh less than the equivalent on a bird of our wristwatches, and ringers must undergo strict training before being awarded the necessary licence.

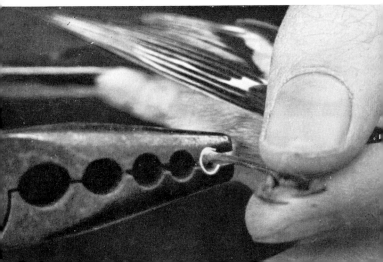

21. A new nature reserve, created in a ballast pit near Sevenoaks, Kent. Note the indented coastline of the islands, and the floating nesting 'raft' in the middle distance.

22. The same scene only two or three years later: the trees and food plants, all specially planted by Dr Harrison and his helpers, have grown well and now hold many more wetland species.

23. *A wedge-shaped nestbox designed for Treecreepers, which normally nest in crevices behind flaps of bark.*

24. *An open-fronted nestbox designed to tempt the Pied Wagtails that are common on Aylesbury sewage farm.*

25. The Heligoland trap in the garden of Skokholm Bird Observatory, off the Pembrokeshire coast. We are looking into the mouth of the funnel, and the catching box is in the middle distance, alongside the wall.

26. Ringers working at mist nets set in a woodland clearing. Note the bird awaiting extraction in the left foreground, and how difficult it is to see the nets stretching well beyond the ringers.

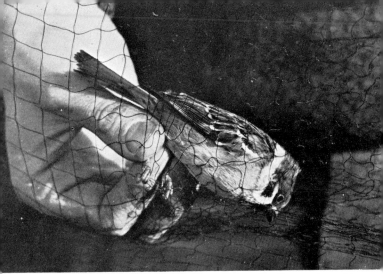

27. A Tree Sparrow is carefully removed from the fine meshes of a mist net. Special training is needed before ringers are allowed to use these very efficient catching techniques.

28. (Below left) A Puffin with a standard numbered ring on its left leg, and with a coloured plastic ring (coded LULU) on its right. Observation through powerful binoculars will show how often Lulu visits her burrow.

29. (Below right) A Puffin with a beakful of food for its youngster — usually 10-20 small fish are caught on each expedition, but catches of more than 40 have occasionally been recorded.

Pied Flycatchers

5. PRACTICAL BIRD WATCHING

Bird biology

What is so special about being a bird? What are their peculiar characteristics? Perhaps the most obvious of these are feathers and the ability to fly. Way back in time the first birds evolved from tree-climbing lizard-like reptiles. Although birds still have some reptilian features, of which the laying of eggs is one of the most important and the scales on the legs and feet one of the more immediately obvious, they, like mammals, developed a greatly improved blood circulatory system and became warm-blooded, enabling them to live much more high-powered lives than the reptiles and amphibians.

Warm-blooded animals must be able to conserve body heat – the mammals use hair, the birds, feathers which have evolved from reptile scales. The nature of feathers varies greatly, from the strong, very stiff wing feathers which can tolerate speeds as fast as a car's, through the rigid tail feathers that serve as a prop to woodpeckers on tree trunks, to the very complex and soft underbody feathers such as Eider-down, more efficient insulators than any man-made cellular clothing. On top of this the feathers must be waterproof, windproof, and durable, for usually they are only changed once or twice a year – a period called moult when old worn feathers fall out and are replaced by new ones to a regular pattern over a period. Often, too, the feathers form a most important part of the bird's ways of attracting a mate, defending its territory, and sometimes in scaring off intruders, and must thus be boldly coloured and patterned.

Flight

Flight itself is a very specialised activity that requires other modifications to a birds' structure in addition to wings. Obviously the weight to be lifted by a given pair of wings must be kept as small as possible, and as there are considerable stresses and strains on the skeleton, bones must be both as strong and as light as possible. Many are hollow tubes, the longer bones with an inside system of cross struts closely resembling a modern girder. As the whole business requires the efficient use of energy, a system of breathing has developed in which the lungs are compact but highly efficient, and which incorporates reservoir air-sacs situated in the body and sometimes in the bigger hollow bones.

The power of flight has opened for birds new areas to exploit for food, and the speed with which fresh feeding areas can be reached has led to the very extensive development of migration. The purpose of migration is relatively clear – it allows freedom of

R.A.H.

Sand Martins – long-distance migrants – mobbing a Buzzard – in Britain a 'partial migrant'

movement to feed and possibly to breed in areas hospitable for only part of the year. The migrations of birds have been studied for many years now and the extraordinary feats of endurance and navigational ability are well known: Swallows, for instance, wintering in South Africa, regularly return to nest in the same barn or porch in Britain in successive years. The young Cuckoo finds its own way to winter quarters in Africa, leaving this country some time *after* the adults have departed. Much as we now know about the summer and winter quarters and much as ringing and the study of migration by radar have shown about the routes taken, we still know relatively little about the mechanisms of orientation, navigation, timing and survival that lie behind such feats – feats only to us, commonplace events to the birds themselves.

Of course different birds fly in very different ways, and the structure of their wings differs accordingly. Most small birds have more or less rounded wings, which give a good deal of 'lift' at take-off, and thus allow a quick getaway from danger, be it a car or a stealthy cat. Such round wings are seen best developed in birds like the Pheasant and Partridge, where avoidance of man is of prime importance. Short round wings are not particularly efficient for extended, or specialised flight. Many of the falcons, such as the Peregrine, which are amongst the fastest fliers, have medium-length, pointed and very strong wings, while some of the hawks – like the Sparrowhawk, have very rounded ones. Falcons secure their prey in open country by a high speed dive, or 'stoop', from above, with only a short chase, while hawks pursue their quarry through the trees where manoeuvrability is of greater importance. Other specialists are the birds that make use of wind or up-currents, thus saving themselves a great deal of effort. At sea the very long narrow wings of the Albatross and the shorter ones of Fulmars and shearwaters are ideal for skimming across the wave troughs, generally slant-wise to the wind. Overland, the long, very broad wings of the Buzzard and Golden Eagle make best use of thermals (currents of rising warm air) or the up-draughts produced by hills, and this technique is seen to best effect in the vultures, which spend long periods soaring, looking for carrion, and whose silhouette seen from below seems to be entirely wing, so small in comparison are the head and tail.

Feeding

Birds must be able to feed rapidly and effectively, and migrants especially must develop some way of storing food energy for use as 'fuel' to power their muscles on long flights. Generally this is done by depositing fat in the body cavity and under the skin: some birds before their departure on the long flight south in autumn may more than double their weight in this way, and achieve this in a very short period – often only a week or two! A layer of fat beneath the skin also helps those birds that stay over the winter to survive, as it gives added insulation to that already provided by the feathers.

There is also a naturally great variety of types of both beaks and feet in birds – both adapted very closely to the way of life. Thus the swimming birds have feet with webs of one sort or another between the toes (penguins also have wings modified to serve as the main means of swimming below water); some of the waders have very long legs (carried to enormous extremes in the

Stilt) to enable them to feed in deeper water; and many of the birds of prey have very powerful feet with long, strong claws. In the case of the Osprey, catching fish, the skin on the soles of the feet resembles coarse glasspaper, giving a good grip on slippery prey, and it is not often realised how long are the legs of predators like the Barn Owl. The long-toed feet of many waders and birds like the Water Rail and Moorhen also help to distribute the weight well on soft mud or floating water plants, stopping the bird sinking straight in. The tree-climbers, like woodpeckers, have feet and claws almost resembling the birds of prey as they need a good grip on the bark, but in the case of the woodpeckers additionally adapted in that, instead of the usual three toes forward, one back, they are arranged two and two, which allows greater manoeuvrability.

The range of beaks is almost as great – we have already seen the variety in the waders, and how many are adapted to feeding in one particular way in one region – occupying a 'niche' – ranging from the long, curved beak of the Curlew through the chisel of the Oystercatcher to the shovel of the Turnstone. The flesh-eating birds of prey all have strongly hooked beaks for tearing flesh, whilst some of the fish-eaters, like the Gannet or the Heron, have long dagger-like beaks and flexible necks, making swift thrusts to secure their prey. Most seed-eaters have short, stout and usually strong triangular beaks for crushing open seeds, fruit or nuts to reach the energy-rich interior. Perhaps the most powerfully developed of all in Britain is the Hawfinch, which can crack open damson stones to reach the kernel, and which is said to be able to exert a pressure of 200 pounds per square inch with its bill! Insect-eaters on the other hand show rather more variety, from the very fine pointed, down-curved beaks of the Wren or the Treecreeper, designed for searching cracks in bark and so on for small insects or their eggs, to the robust chisel of the Great Spotted Woodpecker, designed to cut a way into timber to reach burrowing insects and their larvae using the barbed tip of its long tongue to extract them. The Green Woodpecker is also primarily an insectivorous bird, specialising in feeding on ants, which it reaches with an extraordinarily long tongue, copiously covered in sticky saliva. It inserts its tongue into the ants' galleries, having broken into the anthill with its beak.

The study of bird biology and the many adaptations that birds show to varying environments and ways of life forms a large subject which space does not allow to be fully investigated here. Perhaps this section can best be closed by an outline of the bird's year and the principal events during it.

The bird's year

Winter represents a time of severe stress – temperatures are low, food scarce and daylight (and thus feeding time) short – and for most birds the main concern is with remaining alive. Early spring sees the departure of winter visitors for the north, the arrival of the earliest of our summer visitors and the beginning for most species of the preliminaries, such as courtship and territorial activity, to the breeding season. As spring progresses, so all the winter visitors have departed, and even late-comers like the Spotted Flycatcher and Swift have arrived from Africa to breed here. Nests are built, eggs are laid and young reared, sometimes only one brood and sometimes several, depending both on the species of bird and on the season. This again must be a period of stress – a territory to defend for the male, eggs to produce (perhaps half her own weight or more) for the female, and ultimately several voracious and growing mouths to feed. At the end of the breeding season comes the major moult for most species, when the adults change all their feathers, while the young usually change only the body feathers, not the flight ones. For species that are to stay the winter, there is reasonable time for this process, but for the summer visitors, the time of departure

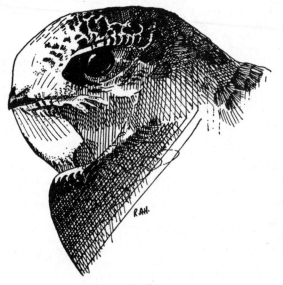

Swift

for winter quarters to the south is fast approaching and the moult must essentially be a speedy operation. In the Whitethroat, for example, moult is completed in about a month, during which time fat is also accumulated for the southward migration, whereas for the smaller but resident Blue Tit, moulting alone occupies nearly four months. And so the days shorten again, and the first Fieldfares herald autumn or wild geese the winter, and the many birds that seek the relative warmth of our oceanic winter (in contrast to the very cold continental one) arrive.

Bird study

The association of amateur birdwatchers with the scientific study, ornithology, is a very long-standing one, and in ornithology as in many other biological fields we owe a considerable debt to the devoted amateurs (generally in times when life was run at a rather more leisurely pace) who have laid the foundation of our knowledge. In many respects bird watching lends itself to this: interest in birds is widespread, they are fairly conspicuous and of a sufficient size to be fairly easily observed and counted (compared, for example, with inconspicuous creatures like snakes or mice). Furthermore, the widely based information that can be gathered by a network of observers blends well with the sort of intensive research projects carried out within, say, universities.

Although in existence in the last century, it is really since the early 1900s that organised surveys of birds have come into their own, to be followed more recently by a chain of more detailed associated biological studies, many based on the numbers of birds caught and ringed each year. Much of this type of bird study is organised on a regional basis by local societies, who produce projects for their members from time to time, but national surveys are almost entirely organised by one of four bodies, the Royal Society for the Protection of Birds (RSPB), the Wildfowl Trust, the Irish Wildbird Conservancy and the British Trust for Ornithology (BTO), whose addresses can be found on pages 90–91.

The RSPB, although primarily a reserve-owning and educational conservation body, has, especially through its junior wing, the Young Ornithologists' Club (YOC), a continuous series of enquiries under way. Perhaps the most important of these at the moment, designed for all members, is the Beached Bird Survey, run in conjunction with the Seabird Group. This was started many years ago in an attempt to assess the quantity of seabirds perishing annually due to oil pollution of the sea, and subsequently washed up on our beaches. Observers are asked to return a count of oiled birds for a stretch of coastline walked at regular intervals through the year, but supplementary counts are always useful. By this means a check can be kept on areas where pollution is unusually heavy, or the kill from specific incidents (like the wreck of the *Torrey Canyon* off the Scilly Isles in 1967) can be assessed and compared with other incidents both in Britain and Ireland and elsewhere in Europe. At a time like the present, when many seabirds – especially the auks – are suffering severe losses each year from oil pollution (plate 2), it is difficult to exaggerate the importance of these results in discussions of the necessity to introduce stricter methods of limiting oil discharge at sea.

Guillemots – the nearer bird is the 'bridled' form

Wildfowl counts

The Wildfowl Trust has also already been mentioned because of the conservational and educational value of its network of reserves and refuges. They also have one major field study – a continuing one, with a long history and correspondingly great value – in which practical birdwatchers participate. This is the monthly wintertime duck count. In a specified period each month the various species of ducks, geese and swans on both coastal and inland sites are counted, and in this way fluctuations in their numbers either due to the success of the breeding season (often poor for those species like Brent Geese breeding in somewhat savage conditions north of the Arctic Circle) or due to shooting pressure. In North America the annual allowable bag of wildfowl is governed by biologists using census and ringing data. In Britain especially, and elsewhere in western Europe, perhaps a greater threat than shooting exists in the numerous proposals to place barrages across bays or estuaries. In the Netherlands this threat is now a reality, and whilst the process of forming polders produces areas very rich in a great variety of birds, especially wildfowl and waders, the ultimate goal, stretches of arable farmland, are very dull indeed for the birdwatcher. Against this background, the enjoyment for the birdwatcher of days spent amongst ducks and geese can be turned to very real conservation benefit.

The BTO, which in Ireland works in close association with the Irish Wildbird Conservancy, is the one organisation specially founded by birdwatchers to co-ordinate their bird watching activities and studies, and consequently the very great majority of today's practical bird watching studies are organised and administered through the Trust's headquarters in Tring, Hertfordshire. The group of enthusiasts who founded the BTO in 1932 could hardly have foreseen how successful in so many fields the organisation was to become, nor how valuable both to biology and to conservation.

Censuses

Many of the early BTO enquiries were into the distribution and numbers of single species of birds; one of the first concerned the Heron and this census is still carried out annually in heronries across the country. In consequence the Heron's is one of the best-documented bird populations in the world, and this information is now proving specially valuable, as the Heron, at the head of a food chain, is currently suffering from the largely unforeseen effects of some agricultural chemicals, and it is possible to look at the changing population figures with a knowledge of the species' ability to recover, for example, from the effects of a severe winter. Periodically, surveys have been conducted of both breeding and wintering gulls – perhaps problem species of the not too distant future and certainly economically important already (plate 17) – and on the smaller birds of prey – again suffering at the hands of modernised farming, agrochemicals and man. In a way the Great Crested Grebe has been a success story – persecuted for its feathers but relieved of this pressure by changes both in the law and in fashion, it flourished greatly on the expanding network of ballast and clay pits that our modern rate of building demands, only recently to fall foul, as does the Heron, of accumulating organochlorine pesticide residues in our waterways: this is another species very suitable for regular censuses.

Regrettably few surveys of this nature can have a happy ending – the declines of the Red-backed Shrike (the beautiful 'butcher bird', impaling its prey on thorns or barbed wire) and the Wryneck, a rare relative of the woodpeckers, have been followed, but little, it seems, can be done to reverse these particular declines. Similarly the gradually accelerating decline of the Corncrake, largely due to the introduction of more sophisticated methods of producing and harvesting hay, is one apparently unlikely to be reversed. The Corncrake is now mainly a bird of Ireland and the Western Isles of Scotland.

When in the late 1950s pigeon-fanciers complained that Peregrine Falcons were killing too many of their homing and racing birds, the Home Office, through the Nature Conservancy, asked the BTO to organise a breeding season survey to assess the position. Several hundred birdwatchers helped a small team of professional ornithologists in 1961 and 1962. The startling results produced a shock reaction that in many ways remains the cornerstone of the fight against environmental pollution – a fight that regrettably must still continue at ever-increasing intensity. Far from expanding to problem proportions, the Peregrine population was shown to have dwindled greatly, and worse still, the surviving pairs were not nesting or rearing young successfully – a very gloomy outlook for the future. Subsequent research revealed the nature of the biological upsets – those females that were breeding laid thin-shelled eggs – very prone to accidental damage during incubation, or to 'cannibalistic' egg-eating by the female herself – a behavioural problem associated with the production of thin-shelled eggs in several bird species. Close investigation of shell thickness by Dr D. A. Ratcliffe showed a sudden very marked, reduction about 1946, the time that DDT, a versatile insecticide developed during the Second World War, was released on to the agricultural chemical market. Only quite recently has the extreme persistence (the length of life of the chemical in the environment) of DDT and related insecticides been fully realised and the mechanisms of concentration in food chains understood. There are now world-wide moves to ban or limit the use of this type of chemical, and research is in progress to find satisfactory substitutes. Pilot surveys indicate that the voluntary restrictions on use that have been in force in Britain for some years may at last be having a good effect: the population of Peregrines is on the increase, and breeding success is also rising.

The problems of environmental pollution are very difficult to resolve satisfactorily on a world-wide basis. Whilst in Britain we deplore the recent use of large quantities of DDT and other persistent pesticides and the slow progress that has been made in replacing them with more satisfactory materials, it is impossible to argue against the use of DDT (a cheap and easily applied substance) in malaria-ridden tropical countries. Undoubtedly also in areas where starvation threatens, crop increases due to DDT have saved many thousands of human lives. Our increasing understanding of this sort of problem demonstrates the value of bird watching to mankind in general.

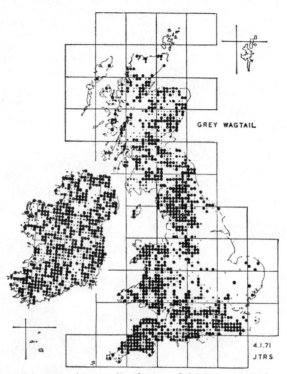

Atlas map showing distribution of the Grey Wagtail

A bird atlas

One of the most exciting projects – and certainly the largest co-operative effort ever by amateur naturalists – has been the preparation by the BTO of an *Ornithological Atlas of Britain and Ireland.* Our islands are divided into more than 3,800 10-kilometre squares by the National Grid which is marked on all Ordnance Survey maps, and during the five-year study period 1968–72, birdwatchers visited all of these, recording in them species possibly, probably or certainly breeding. The interim map for the Grey Wagtail shows just how widespread this bird has become after its recovery from very low numbers after the savage 1962–3 winter. The finished atlas is going to be an immensely valuable inventory of our breeding birds, a Domesday Book for the conservationist, and a source of endless help and information to birdwatchers who want to know where birds are. Subsequent studies will be taking birdwatchers into the fields of ecology, attempting to examine the distribution patterns and why birds occur where they do – a fascinating prospect of several years' enjoyable field work for the birdwatcher of today and tomorrow. For many species, or in smaller areas (say the size of a county) a finer grid is going to be necessary, and some of the county societies have used 2×2 kilometre squares (tetrads) — these allow a much closer association of bird with habitat on a local scale. This map shows very clearly the coastal (and Bodmin Moor) distribution of the Stonechat in Cornwall — far more informatively than the 10-kilometre squares. In the future, perhaps twenty years' time, we shall be able to repeat the whole atlas, measuring and assessing changes, and plans are already afoot to cover all Europe.

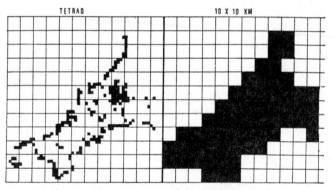

TETRAD   10 X 10 KM

Map showing the distribution of the Stonechat in Cornwall

Estuary counts

Closely parallel to the wildfowl counts, the BTO/RSPB Birds of Estuaries Survey seeks to quantify the numbers of birds, especially waders, using our estuaries, and the times when they use them. Of our presently available habitats, estuaries are one of the most limited in quantity and most threatened by development, which may be of one or a combination of several types, but all schemes depend on throwing a dam or barrage across the estuary mouth, thereby removing all the desirable features of an estuary, which are dependent on a combination of the ecological richnesses of both a river and the sea. Developmental pressures may demand the use of the estuary as an industrialised port (perhaps complete with London's third airport) (plate 18), for reservoirs, water for recreational purposes, or reclamation for farming. It is most important that we know which of our estuaries are the most important – whether they carry large numbers of several species or whether they are vital to just one species – perhaps a rare one like the Avocet. The problem has international aspects, too. Our estuaries are very important as 'staging posts' for birds breeding in the brief summer of the Arctic, and migrating to the Mediterranean or Africa for the winter months. On our estuaries they gather, making use of the very rich food supply to moult and then to put on layers of reserve fat to serve as 'fuel' on the long journey south.

Garden birds

From asking the question 'how important are our estuaries?' can we turn to asking 'how important are our gardens?' in maintaining the populations of many of the small birds that are so much part of our lives. Feeding garden birds is now becoming an everyday happening in many homes (plate 19). How many birds are dependent on this and how quickly do they acquire the habit of coming to the bird-table? Are there some species that will not be tempted at all – no matter what is put out for them? Are the numbers of birds in the garden indicative of population levels as a whole, and do they fluctuate in much the same way as the whole 'wild' population? These are some of the questions that the Garden Bird Feeding Survey and similar studies set out to answer. One example will help to illustrate the potential importance of gardens to bird populations during hard times: in a north London area, where most Blackbirds are very largely dependent on the food put out for them by housewives, weights during a fortnight-long snowy spell averaged about 140 grams - a good winter weight for this species. Within thirty miles of London, in a woodland nature reserve, during the same cold period, Blackbird weights quickly fell to between 80 and 90 grams, approaching starvation levels – because the snow cover on the ground prevented normal feeding and no other foods were available. Fortunately that cold spell ended before very many deaths had occurred, but this will not always be the case.

Common Birds Census

Another fascinating but more detailed study, designed to show us how our modern environment puts pressures on them, is the

Common Birds Census. In this, birdwatchers all over Britain and Ireland visit their census areas (usually from 60–300 acres in extent) between ten and twenty times each breeding season, and on each visit mark on a large-scale map the position of birds showing any form of behaviour (such as singing, fighting or nest-building) associated with territory-holding or breeding. At the end of the season, tracings are made of the daily visit maps, and the records are seen to fall into well-defined groups, each group indicating the territory of a pair of birds. The number of territories can be counted and compared with the previous year's figure, and if this process is repeated on many census areas, an accurate 'population index' can be calculated showing how various species are coping. The census, CBC for short, was originally started on farmland areas to investigate changes in common bird populations due to new agrochemicals or new farming techniques, but it has now been extended to cover woodland as well. In many respects it provides our only means of assessing changes in bird populations in an area when, for example, a new housing or industrial estate is built (strangely this is not *always* a bad thing!) or when a farmer removes all his hedgerows. In itself this becomes completely absorbing as you follow the changes in an area of land, but against a national background the pooled individual contributions provide reliable figures, and reliable figures are what conservationists must have if they are to stem the flood of development and modernisation that, in some respects, jeopardises our countryside. Like the toxic chemicals situation, this argument can never be entirely one-sided, but the strength of vested developmental interests is such that the conservationist needs a good armament of facts if he is to receive a hearing at all.

More and more now, CBC workers are looking at nature reserves and other recreational or conservation areas to see what birds they support, to study the effects of vegetation changes and to devise where possible the most effective usage and future management plans. All too often areas may be tacitly assumed to be 'wasteland' in need of a good cleaning up, whereas if these areas (for example disused railway lines) are properly managed they may become oases of bird populations in a farmland desert. Wide expanses of mown grass, with occasional trees, may give the impression of areas for recreation, but possess few of the charms of the countryside. So the field for the new worker is wide, and the needs great. Recent work, especially by Dr Jeffery Harrison in Kent, is showing just how effective amateur enthusiasm can be in *creating* habitat for birds – his wetland reserve near Sevenoaks will be a model for many years to come (plates 21, 22). On a smaller scale, the provision of nestboxes (see page

80) for any species helps, but those for species whose nest sites are threatened – such as Barn Owls and Kestrels – may be specially valuable.

Nesting birds

Another line of practical bird watching which, like the Garden Bird Feeding Survey, is available to all – even those fairly closely tied to their own gardens – is the study of nests, nesting behaviour and success. When we come to understand how a bird population works, or to decide what conservation measures are necessary for a particular species, obviously we must have a good working knowledge of the sort of habitat it prefers for breeding and feeding, where and when it builds its nests, how many young are raised, how many nests fail and what are the causes of failure – the weather, cats, humans (regrettably) and so on. The Nest Record Scheme of the BTO gathers together these types of information from all over the country. As it was started before the war, and currently receives 20,000 or more records of nests each year, its store of facts is most valuable, and is extensive enough to allow comparison of success rates now with those of some time ago. Standard cards are used to record information like the duration of nest building, the date of laying the first egg, the clutch size and incubation period, the fledging period and the overall success of the nest. Many of these facts can be gathered by a planned series of visits – for the most minutely detailed study less than one visit a day is needed – so that disturbance of the bird is kept to a minimum. The Wildlife and Countryside Act provides protection for nearly all nests, with special protection for rarer species, but with all nests the cardinal rule is *always put the birds' interests first!*

Most individuals of nearly all species are very tolerant of nest inspections but great care must be taken not to reveal the whereabouts of the nest to marauding children or other predators by leaving a trampled trail through the vegetation. Incidentally, birds have next to no sense of smell, and will not be able to detect your visit in this way. Some may be specially sensitive around the period when they are building the nest and when the eggs are hatching, so visits should be brief and kept to a minimum at these times. Possibly even more important, well-feathered young may use their predator-escape mechanism and 'explode' from the nest if disturbed; whilst this may save some of them from cats, others will undoubtedly perish, lost in the undergrowth where their parents cannot find or feed them, so this must be avoided at all costs. For most nests at this stage, viewing from a distance is quite adequate to provide the information you need. The BTO publishes a *Guide to the Nest Record Scheme* which gives full details of the recording techniques, with hints on how and when to find nests and a full guide to the 'dos' and 'don'ts' of nest finding.

Nestboxes

A logical extension of nest recording, and one well suited especially to the birdwatcher whose movements are rather more restricted, is a study of one or several of the species which uses nestboxes or other artificial nest sites. Part of the fascination of nestboxes lies in the confiding nature of most of the species using them, and in the intimate detail in which the study can be carried out. Tits – especially Blue and Great – are probably the most frequent users of nestboxes in all types of surroundings including town gardens, but another fascinating, and often taxing aspect of this sort of bird watching is trying to tempt other less usual species to use artificial sites (plates 23, 24). This is greatly aided by a knowledge of the natural nesting habits of the desired species. One example of the sort of information that a nestbox study will provide is brood sizes in town and country for Blue Tits:

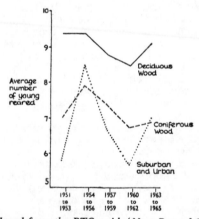

Reproduced from the BTO guide 'Nest Record Scheme'

As for the Nest Record Scheme, the BTO publishes a booklet *Nestboxes* (one design is shown here), which not only gives details of how to carry out such a study, but also of the design, construction, siting and protection of a whole variety of nestbox types for tits, flycatchers, sparrows, Starling, Jackdaw, owls, Kestrel and so on.

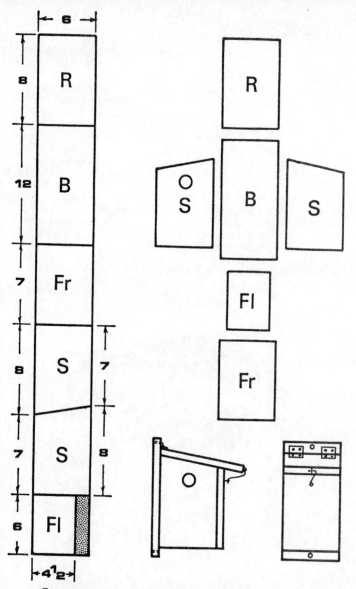

*Construction of a nestbox suitable for small hole-nesters
such as blue tits (reproduced from the BTO guide 'Nestboxes')*

Some of the predatory species that regularly use nestboxes, and most other raptors, produce pellets composed of the indigestible remains of their prey – bones, feathers and fur. By this means the various items of prey taken can be identified, and if pellets are collected from around the nest and from winter roosts in thickets, old buildings and so on, the change of diet with season can be investigated. Similarly differences in diet between species can be studied – how much does the Little Owl depend on insects, and how much on mammals and birds? In one area in Kent, for example, Little Owls will even tackle birds as big as Mistle Thrushes, and in the same place Long-eared Owls are as dependent on hunting small birds as they are on voles and mice. Jointly with the BTO, the Mammal Society is producing a booklet on prey identification from pellet analyses. Most of these predatory species, after long and in some cases regrettably continuing persecution by gamekeepers, are now suffering more from a reduction in suitable habitat and from the cumulative effects of toxic agrochemicals, so any understanding of their food requirements could be to their benefit. Occasionally examination of an owl or hawk pellet will reveal a numbered metal bird ring, from the leg of a bird that has formed part of the predator's diet.

Tawny Owl

Ringing

Historically, ringing started at the end of the last century in Denmark, and two schemes started in Britain in 1909, merging in 1937, to be administered by the BTO. Now many European countries have organised schemes, with an international co-operative body, Euring, arranging for the use of standard techniques and forms. With automatic data processing facilities available, it is important that national records can be exchanged and processed elsewhere. In North America, similar schemes govern bird 'banding', as it is known there, often organised by the Fish and Wildlife Services, but one privately run station in Ontario, Canada, uses rings carrying a biblical text.

Birds are very delicate creatures and easily damaged by rough or incorrect handling. All bird ringers undergo an extensive training by experts before receiving a licence from the Nature Conservancy to ring on their own. Besides this, in Britain they must have a permit from the BTO, who administer the National Ringing Scheme. Quite obviously none of the techniques – usually nets or traps – used to catch birds for ringing causes them any harm, nor do the birds seem unduly disturbed by handling. Indeed, some garden ringers have trouble from birds so accustomed to traps and handling that the 'free meal' provided tempts them time after time on the same day!

Each bird caught is marked with an individually numbered metal ring (plate 20), made of lightweight alloy (650 of the smallest weigh less than an ounce) – and relatively speaking weighing less than your watch. Thus each has its own number – rather like a motor-car registration plate, and also stamped on the ring is an address to which the finder returns details of recovery. This is either the internationally understood 'British Museum (Nat. Hist.) London, SW7' or, on the smallest sizes 'BTO, Tring, England'. Nowadays over half a million birds are ringed in Britain each year, and some 14,000 recovered.

Catching birds

Many migrants are caught at the network of coastal bird observatories (see page 56), in large, funnel-shaped wire-netting traps (plate 25) called 'Heligolands' after the famous island observatory in the North Sea where the design was perfected. These are usually built over a line of bushes, and from an entrance up to 40 feet wide by 10 feet high narrow rapidly until only a glass-fronted box awaits the birds. Seeing this apparent exit, the birds head towards it, only to find themselves confined in a catching box from which the ringer can take them for ringing. However, since the 1950s, catching migrants (and other birds) has been made much easier for ringers by the introduction from

Japan of 'mist nets' (plate 26). These nets, which are very fine but strong nylon or terylene mesh, almost as fine as hair-nets (plate 27), suspended on stronger cross strands, can be set against a background of vegetation where they are practically invisible to birds in flight. Their easy portability and versatility is causing them to replace most other forms of catching birds. Obviously their sale and operation is most strictly controlled to prevent misuse. Garden birds are caught either using mist nets or in a variety of small traps (derived from traps used by the bird-catchers in years gone by), of which the simplest is basically a sieve propped up by a stick with a length of string attached. Once the bird is under the sieve, the string is pulled – and the bird is caught.

Migration

The first use of ringing was to determine the destinations and the routes taken by some of our migrants, and for many the maps are now beginning to fill up. For some though, the picture is just reaching a tantalising stage: the Lesser Whitethroat, it appears, migrates southwards to the region of the Sudan in autumn via

Knot

Italy and Egypt. Returning to this country in spring, the route seems further to the east, northwards through Israel and the Lebanon, before turning west, probably passing across Europe north of the Alps.

Some of the really spectacular results so far produced concern the long-distance migration routes of some of our seabirds. Manx Shearwaters winter off the coasts of Brazil, Argentina and Uruguay, and can manage the 6,000-mile trip from their breeding islands off the coast of Wales in as little as a fortnight! Recently a British-ringed Manx Shearwater was washed ashore in the Great Australian Bight; Kittiwakes and Fulmars disperse widely across the Atlantic, while skuas, petrels and terns spread south of the equator. Arctic Terns have been caught on whaling ships on the edge of the Antarctic pack-ice – a fantastic movement each migration season, and one incidentally which gives them almost continuous maximum day-length, as winter here is summer in the southern hemisphere. For sheer speed, a Knot – an Arctic-breeding wader – ringed on southward autumn passage on the Wash and recovered in West Africa only eight days later must take some beating.

The bird navigational feat of all time was performed by a Manx Shearwater (ring number AX 6587) from the breeding colony on Skokholm Bird Observatory off Pembrokeshire. AX 6587 was flown (by commercial airliner) to Boston, USA, over 3,000 miles away. Just twelve and a half days later it had safely returned to its nesting burrow on the island, beating the letter from America giving details of the date and time of its release by a short head.

The experiments that early ornithologists like Audubon in the USA carried out using coloured threads on the legs of Swallows have now been frequently repeated with metal rings, especially on small birds. The results today are similar to those obtained by the early workers: adult birds of many species like the warblers and the Stonechat and Whinchat will return with great precision year after year to the same areas, and even to the same clump of bushes in the case of warblers, or barn, garage or porch in the case of the Swallow. For other species, though, the pattern is more variable. Lapwings, Redwings and Fieldfares may winter in western Europe – even in Ireland – one year, and in south-eastern Europe the next. Within the continent of Europe, different populations or races of the same species may show quite different trends. Continental populations of many thrushes and finches are strongly migratory, while their British counterparts are quite sedentary. Sometimes this may be associated with climatic severity: for example populations of thrushes, sedentary in southern England, are migratory in northern England and

Scotland where the cold winters force them to be.

In many cases, the use of rings to discover wintering areas or to plot migration routes has now taken a secondary place to other studies. For several species, sufficient are recovered each year to allow an annual 'mortality' assessment, which can be balanced against the 'productivity' assessed from the Nest Records Scheme. Ringing studies reveal the very considerable life spans of some species once the perils of the first year of life have been overcome, and all this information is of great value to the biologist designing plans for conservation. I have already mentioned that in the USA, for example, the mortality figures for ducks and geese are used, together with the previous season's breeding performance figures, to set a reasonable 'bag' limit for hunters, and to determine the length of the shooting season.

The catching efficiency of mist nets means that large samples of bird populations can be caught, and that individual birds may be re-trapped frequently. Here the ring is used to identify the individual, so that its life history may be closely followed. Much the same result can be obtained using combinations of coloured plastic rings (plate 28), which for some population dynamics studies remove the need to catch the bird again.

The study of weights is one such: the Blackbirds mentioned in the Garden Bird Feeding Survey were caught and weighed by ringers, and weight is one good guide to the health of the bird. Other similar studies of migrants have shown how Reed Warblers put on relatively little fat in autumn for use as 'fuel' on the flight south, which is made in easy stages, while Sedge Warblers may more than double their weight before making the journey to Africa – very possibly in one hop. The distribution of ringing recoveries supports this theory.

During ringing, when birds are being handled, their state of moult can be recorded. Previously rather little was known about this biologically important aspect of a bird's life – important because of the drain on energy to produce a complete set of new feathers – but regular retrapping allows an assessment of the rate of moult.

The origins of birds caught up in major disasters – especially the seabirds involved in the oiling incident following the wreck of the *Torrey Canyon* or the many species that died during the 1962–3 winter – can only be determined from ringing recoveries. Coincidentally, recoveries do provide one means of making a reasonable quantitative assessment of the magnitude of the disaster. On this basis the 'wreck' of auks in the Irish Sea in autumn 1969, when many thousands of dead birds were washed ashore, and for which the cause is not yet fully explained, was on a considerably greater scale than the *Torrey Canyon* disaster (plate 2). Recoveries can also reveal some very unsatisfactory aspects of bird protection in this country: as an example, of the few Osprey chicks reared in Scotland under careful and costly protection by the RSPB, some have been shot in southern Europe, where conservation is not such an active enthusiasm. The terrible tolls taken by the bird-catchers of Belgium, France, Cyprus, Malta and Italy are also revealed in the number of recoveries reported as 'taken' or 'shot' during the autumn passage.

Rarities

There are other aspects of bird watching where communication between birdwatchers is essential – so far we have discussed topics mainly concerned with bird biology or with conservation, but the accurate identification of the bird in the first place is important. Just as your own ability will increase greatly with practice, the rare birds that occur in this country become more easily recognisable if we can refer to useful field descriptions. Often such a description is based as much on the behaviour of the bird, its actions, its attitudes and so on – called by bird-watchers its 'jizz' – as on details of its plumage. You will find that if you make notes when you see particular birds for the first few times, references to these allows you to refresh your memory, and gradually the job becomes easier. For real rarities, these field notes are vital. With them you can confirm your identification from books, and you may have found new aspects of behaviour that if written down could be of great help to others.

Behaviour

Behaviour studies are a tremendously interesting topic – how do birds react to various situations – even to each other. There is still much to learn, and from many common species, even of behaviour on the bird-table: does, for example, the type of food that is offered affect which species is dominant? I do not know. How many garden birds flock together in winter, which species, and are the flocks all of one sex? Sometimes rings or colour rings are necessary to answer these questions, but often only close observation will provide the answers. One additional problem here is passing on your findings to others – it is extremely difficult to write briefly and with lucid precision on this sort of topic. Both here and with field descriptions, never hesitate to make field sketches, however rough. They are almost always helpful, and if you have a smattering of ability, may be very valuable indeed as well as most enjoyable in the drawing.

One way out of this is to use a camera with a telephoto lens to record what you see – bird's attitudes to one another and so on. Too often today a camera is still used largely to photograph birds at the nest rather than to record aspects of everyday bird life – gathering food, bathing, anting, sun-bathing, competing for space, gathering nest material, looking after young *after* they have fledged. Only one or two specialist photographers have made any inroads on this field, which is really ripe now for exploitation by amateur enthusiasts.

Much the same can be said of tape recordings, now that adequate portable recorders are quite cheaply available. We need to know far more of the calls (rather than the song) of many species, and in some cases the great possibilities of looking at regional variations in the song of a single species are only just being explored. The Society of Wildlife Recordists exists to foster this sort of exercise and to encourage exchange and co-operation with tapes.

Through this chapter I hope that one or two main threads have become apparent – perhaps the most important of these to the newcomer actually looking at birds, watching them with an interested intent, is that there is still very much to learn. Another point: while both for pleasure and to gain the widest experience to increase our expertise, visits to all sorts of habitats are strongly recommended, there comes a time when a series of visits to one place regularly through the year can be even more interesting to the birdwatcher himself as well as yielding much more of the sort of information on birds that we need if we are interested in their numbers, lives and conservation. This brings me to my final point in this chapter: I hope that I have shown that the birdwatcher has a very real, and sometimes vital, contribution to make to understanding birds and their ways of life. So much has stemmed from our interests in the past (for example the Peregrine Survey) that has a very immediate relevance to the present (concern over pesticides and other materials polluting our environment). Not only do I suggest that this lends additional interest and zest to our bird watching, it removes absolutely none of the enjoyment while contributing greatly to the understanding that we must nowadays have as a basis for conservation.

6. CLUBS AND SOCIETIES AND THEIR WORK

We are very fortunate to have in Britain not only a well-knit group of national societies working in harmony but also a very wide choice of organisations at a county level and also in many cities, towns and even villages. Between them they should be able to cater for all tastes, all levels of expertise, and all desires for involvement.

One of the problems for newcomers to any district is to find the nearest club or society: the problem is greathst for the smaller town or village clubs, but the local library may be able to help. Most of these clubs and natural history societies, and most county bird watching or ornithological societies organise a series of varied winter lectures and an all-year-round programme of field outings, where the best local sites and the birds that frequent them can be shown to newcomers. This remains one of the best introductions to bird watching available. Usually too, these clubs and societies produce annual reports on the birds seen in their area, and many of them produce a monthly bulletin giving up-to-the-minute news. In general the **Council for Nature** (c/o The Regents Park Zoological Gardens, London NW1) serves as the co-ordinating body for natural history societies and is the best source of addresses in case of difficulty. *The Shell Bird Book* by James Fisher contains a county-by-county list of clubs, and of regional bird books.

While clubs and societies such as these cater for the instruction and entertainment of the birdwatcher, there are others which, while also serving these functions, regard their main objects to lie more in owning or managing land as nature reserves. Owning a nature reserve carries several responsibilities – one of which may be to protect the wildlife in it *even* from natural history enthusiasts. This point must always be sympathetically remembered when a permit to enter a reserve is difficult to obtain. Membership of such a society *does not automatically confer right of entry* to its reserves, and the instructions of the society or its wardens must always be absolutely observed. It may seem strange, but with the popularity of field excursions, even a nature trail may wear out! Reserves may be created for several purposes – to preserve an area of land of unusual quality, vegetation, bird or animal community; to protect one or two specially threatened species; or to use particularly rich or interesting habitats as a means of educating and encouraging interest in the environment.

There are several national organisations owning reserves of interest to the birdwatcher.

The Nature Conservancy (19 Belgrave Square, London SW1) is the governmental body which owns or manages huge acreages of reserves of biological interest. These reserves are administered through a series of regional offices, and in many cases illustrated leaflets are available on the reserves. Many reserves have wardens to guide and assist visitors.

The National Trust (42 Queen Anne's Gate, London SW1), while concerned with buildings and places of natural beauty, itself maintains and provides wardens for many nature reserves, especially in coastal areas, and in most of the plantations of the **Forestry Commission** (25 Saville Row, London W1X 2AY) access is allowed along the pathways where good views of many of the birds of large woodland areas can be obtained. Particularly in woodland or forest areas, avoid any risk of starting a fire – 'No Smoking' is a *must*!

Many counties now have a County Trust for Nature Conservation: concerned with several other aspects of natural history, besides birds, they own reserves of all sizes within the county. The 'parent body' or association of county trusts is the **Royal Society for Nature Conservation** (The Green, Nettleham, Lincolnshire) from whom details of your own trust can be obtained.

Perhaps the one bird watching society that goes furthest in catering for two aspects of bird watching – conservation and education – is the **Royal Society for the Protection of Birds** (The Lodge, Sandy, Bedfordshire). Owners of many reserves specifically oriented towards both bird protection and conservation, the RSPB rely on their membership to produce funds for their activities and to give weight to their lobby for bird protection and conservation measures. Members may apply for permits to visit reserves, which offer good viewing opportunities for many of our birds – some difficult to find elsewhere. The reserves are wardened and in some cases special facilities are provided to explain the workings of the environment or special features of the ecology of the particular reserve. The RSPB produces an illustrated magazine *Birds* every two months, with current affairs, news of reserves, and articles of general bird watching interest. A network of local branches is being developed.

The film unit produces two or three bird films of an exceptional standard each year – these are shown at regional meetings and subsequently are very popular for hire by other societies. The youth wing of the RSPB is called the **Young Ornithologists' Club,** with a magazine *Bird Life,* field meetings organised by local organisers, and a variety of relatively simple studies in which younger members can participate.

The **Wildfowl Trust** (Slimbridge, Gloucestershire) has very much the same ideals and aims as the RSPB, but restricts its field of interest to wildfowl – ducks, geese and swans. Besides maintaining a network of reserves – especially necessary as refuges in areas where wildfowling might otherwise take an excessive toll – the Wildfowl Trust possesses another exciting and valuable asset – its collections. Here wildfowl can be seen at close quarters and many of the problems of identification can be resolved in comfort. Again special services are offered to junior members, and considerable effort is concentrated on education and instilling an understanding of the place of wildfowl in the modern environment and the often adverse effects of the modern environment on birds.

Within their respective countries, the **Scottish Ornithologists'
Club** (21 Regent Terrace, Edinburgh 7) and the **Irish Wildbird
Conservancy** (c/o Royal Irish Academy, 19 Dawson Street,
Dublin 2) serve many of the functions described above for the
RSPB and the Wildfowl Trust as well as co-operating with the
BTO in national enquiries and organising their own regional
studies of bird populations. **The Seabird Group** (c/o Zoology
Department, University of Aberdeen) caters for all those inter-
ested in the seabirds of Britain and Ireland.

It is to the **British Trust for Ornithology** (Beech Grove, Tring,
Hertfordshire) that the birdwatcher will turn who feels that his
bird watching, while remaining entirely enjoyable, should
contribute something both to mankind and to the welfare of the
birds that he enjoys. The BTO organises or aids a wide variety of
co-operative studies, well exemplified by most of those described
in Chapter 5. Participation and enthusiastic support is achieved
at all levels, and members also receive a quarterly journal *Bird
Study*, reporting on BTO (and other) findings, and a regular
newsletter. Several paperback booklets assist those participating
in various schemes, and three national and several regional
conferences each year keep members well in touch not only with
all aspects of the Trust's work but with developments in the
field of ornithology in general. This unique co-operation between
amateur enthusiasts and the Trust's staff of professional biologists now forms a major contribution to our understanding of
birds and their environment – which indeed is also *our* environment.

7. A SELECTED BIBLIOGRAPHY

There is an almost overwhelming quantity of books about birds and their biology of which many are travelogues – picturesque or even exciting – but which I have not listed as the choice is so essentially personal. Others are more functionally documentary, dealing with the birds of a region or with a single species or a group of species. Yet more deal with the fascinating wealth of detail that surrounds the business of being a bird, and with the interactions between birds and men. Thus this list cannot be in any way comprehensive – many valuable or interesting books are omitted – but it is aimed at providing a series of jumping-off places, allowing the reader to pursue his own course by scanning the references or bibliographies in the books mentioned. Most should be easily available from a good library, and none should be unobtainable from a county library.

Magazines and journals

Birds: two-monthly journal for RSPB members; popular articles and features, well illustrated.

Bird Study: quarterly journal of the BTO; for the serious birdwatcher wishing to see the results of field studies.

British Birds: monthly; published from Fountains, Park Lane, Blunham, Bedfordshire; all aspects covered for the more serious birdwatcher.

Ibis: quarterly journal of the British Ornithologists Union, the senior ornithological body in Britain; detailed scientific studies reported for the real expert.

Wildfowl: annual journal of the Wildfowl Trust; concentrates on many aspects of the study of water birds; illustrated.

Identification

The Birdlife of Britain; P. Hayman and P. Burton; Mitchell Beazley.

The Birds of Britain and Europe with North Africa and the Middle East; Heinzel, Fitter and Parslow; Collins.

The Birds of the British Isles; Bannerman; 12 vols; Oliver and Boyd.

A Field Guide to the Birds of Britain and Europe; Peterson, Mountford and Hollom; Collins.

The Hamlyn Guide to the Birds of Britain and Europe; Bruun and Singer; Hamlyn.

The Handbook of British Birds; Witherby, Jourdain, Ticehurst and Tucker; 5 vols; H. F. and G. Witherby.

The Popular Handbook of British Birds; P. A. D. Hollom; Witherby.

The Popular Handbook of Rarer British Birds; P. A. D. Hollom; Witherby.
The Shell Guide to the Birds of Britain and Ireland; I. J. Ferguson-Lees, I. Wallis, J. T. R. Sharrock; Michael Joseph.

General interest

Atlas of European Birds; K. H. Voous; Nelson.
Binoculars, Cameras and Telescopes; J. J. M. Flegg; BTO.
Bird; L. and L. Darling; Methuen.
A Bird and its Bush; M. Lister; Phoenix House.
Bird Migration; C. J. Mead; Country Life.
Bird Navigation; G. V. T. Matthews; second edition (also in paperback), Cambridge University Press.
Birds and Woods; W. B. Yapp; Oxford University Press.
Birds of the World; O. Austin and A. Singer; Hamlyn.
The Bird Table Book; T. Soper; David and Charles.
The Birdwatcher's Reference Book; M. Lister; Phoenix House.
Enjoying Ornithology; D. Lack; Methuen.
An Eye for a Bird; E. Hosking; Hutchinson.
How Birds Work; R. Freethy; Blandford Press.
In Search of Birds; J. Flegg; Blandford Press.
The Life of Birds; J. C. Welty; Constable.
Man and Birds; R. K. Murton; Collins, New Naturalist Series.
The Migrations of Birds; J. Dorst; Heinemann.
Nestboxes; J. J. M. Flegg and D. E. Glue; BTO.
The Nest Record Scheme; H. Mayer-Gross; BTO.
Pesticides and Pollution; K. Mellanby; Collins, New Naturalist Series.
Population Studies of Birds; D. Lack; Oxford University Press.
Seabirds; J. Fisher and R. M. Lockley; Collins, New Naturalist Series.
The Shell Bird Book; J. Fisher; Ebury Press and Michael Joseph.
Watching Birds; J. Fisher and J. Flegg; Penguin Books.
Where to Watch Birds; J. Gooders; André Deutsch.
Where to Watch Birds in Europe; J. Gooders; André Deutsch.
The World of Birds; J. Fisher and R. T. Peterson; Macdonald.

Monographs

British Thrushes; E. Simms; Collins.
British Tits; C. Perrins; Collins.
Finches; I. Newton; Collins.
Flight Identification of European Raptors; R. Porter, I. Willis, S. Christiansen and B. Neilsen; Poyser.
The Gannet; B. Nelson; Poyser.
The Greenshank; D. Nethersole-Thompson; Collins (New Naturalist Monograph 5).

The Hawfinch; G. Mountfort; Collins (New Naturalist Monograph 15).

The Heron; F. A. Lowe; Collins (New Naturalist Monograph 11).

The Herring Gull's World; N. Tinbergen; Collins (New Naturalist Monograph 9).

The House Sparrow; J. D. Summers-Smith; Collins (New Naturalist Monograph 19).

The Kingfisher; R. Eastman; Collins.

The Life of the Robin; D. Lack; H. F. and G. Witherby.

The Mystery of the Flamingos; L. Brown; Country Life.

Penguins; J. Sparks and T. Soper; David and Charles.

The Peregrine Falcon; D. Ratcliffe; Poyser.

Population Ecology of Raptors; I. Newton; Poyser.

The Puffin; R. M. Lockley; Dent.

The Redstart; J. Buxton; Collins (New Naturalist Monograph 2).

Shearwaters; R. M. Lockley; Dent.

A Study of Blackbirds; D. W. Snow; George Allen and Unwin.

Swifts in a Tower; D. Lack; Methuen.

Waders; W. Hale; Collins.

The Woodpigeon; R. K. Murton; Collins (New Naturalist Monograph 20).

Records

BBC Records; the Wildlife Series contains bird recordings, again divided on a habitat basis; RED 96 has Welsh birds, RED 103 a large number of woodland birds, summer and winter, RED 109 garden and water birds, etc.; 12-inch 33⅓ r.p.m.

Bird Recognition; an aural index recorded by V. C. W. Lewis on HMV; presented as three volumes, each with three 7-inch 45 r.p.m. discs and an explanatory booklet, again divided (with 15 or 16 species per volume) on a habitat basis; 7 EG 8923–31. Victor C. Lewis has also produced other 12-inch 33⅓ r.p.m. records for HMV: *A Tapestry of British Bird Song*, CLP 1723, sixty-odd species; *Guess the Birds*, XLP 50011, 24 species arranged as a test of skill as well as for entertainment; and, for Marble Arch, *Bird Sounds in Close-up*, two 12-inch records, MAL 1102 and 1316, both with a wide spectrum of about forty species arranged in habitat groupings.

Listen the Birds; produced by the RSPB and the Dutch Society for Bird Protection; recordings by Hans A. Traber and John Kirby; a series (now fourteen in number) of 7-inch 33⅓ r.p.m. discs, each with several related species, or with species common to one type of habitat; EPHT 11–14, and HDV 7–14.

Shell Nature Records; published by Discourses for Shell-Mex and B.P. Ltd.; recorded by Lawrence Shove; this series is based on a habitat classification – marsh and riverside, moor and heath, woodland, etc. – with seven 7-inch 33⅓ r.p.m. records so far; DCL 701–7.

A Field Guide to the Bird Songs of Britain and Europe; by Sture Palmér and Jeffery Boswell. Published in four sets of four cassettes by S. R. Records; SRMK 5021/24.

INDEX

96